Beyond Blame

Beyond Blame

How We Can Succeed by
Breaking the Dependency Barrier

Armstrong Williams

Foreword by Malcolm S. Forbes, Jr.

THE FREE PRESS

New York   London   Toronto   Sydney   Tokyo   Singapore

The Free Press
A Division of Simon & Schuster Inc.
866 Third Avenue, New York, N.Y. 10020

Printed in the United States of America

printing number

1 2 3 4 5 6 7 8 9 0

Text design by Carla Bolte

Library of Congress Cataloging-in-Publication Data

Williams, Armstrong
    Beyond blame : how we can succeed by breaking the
    dependency barrier / Armstrong Williams.
        p.   cm.
ISBN 0–02–935365–3
    1. Afro-American men—Conduct of life.   I. Title.
E185.86.W485   1995
305.38′896073—dc20   95–13618
                                                        CIP

To my mother Thelma, and especially to my deceased father, James S. Williams, my strongest supporters and sternest critics, by whom I have been guided, disciplined, and comforted. Though my father sleeps, he lives in me, for I am as he fashioned me.

Contents

Foreword

by Malcolm S. Forbes, Jr.

We are responsible for our actions. That is the core message of this down-to-earth, compassionate-but-no-nonsense series of letters by commentator Armstrong Williams to a twenty-nine-year-old, inner-city, former street hustler who asked Armstrong for help.

Williams wisely avoids glib generalizations and bromides. He has little immediate use for either liberal or conservative "macro-solutions." He discerningly dissects the characteristics of the social breakdown that the seeker of his succor, a man he calls Brad Howard, represents.

He doesn't romanticize Brad. In fact, he clearly conveys to him his disgust at both what Brad has done and how he has rationalized his behavior (which has occasionally been murderous) in a way that leaves Brad feeling little remorse.

Williams recognizes that saving one's soul is not a sweet, comfortable, feel-good process. He lacerates schools for trying to foster a "feel-good-about-yourself" attitude instead of inculcating in kids the intellectual disciplines and tools they need to succeed. False esteem is a road to ruin and bitterness.

He gives short shrift to inner-city adults who turn a blind eye to the wrongdoings of their children, who demand too little of the young. Affirmative action, Williams makes clear, only exacerbates racial tensions. Even its alleged beneficiaries feel a sense of rage, dissatisfaction.

Williams is no mere scold, however. He makes clear how Brad and others can truly redeem themselves. Williams' compassion is of the genuine but tough-love variety, not the wear-it-on-your-sleeve-but-retreat-to-your-secure-suburb kind.

Much has been and will be made of the fact that Williams is a "Black conservative," as if he were some kind of rare, exotic species, wondrous to behold. Actually, as this book confirms, Williams is part and parcel of the uniquely American tradition of self-improvement and renewal.

The U.S. has experienced serious social "pathologies" before. In the 1820s, for example, per capita consumption of liquor was several times what it is today. Everyone drank—adults, preachers, teachers and kids. By today's standards we were a nation of drunks with all the predictable results. In the late 1820s and early 1830s, there arose a powerful social reaction to this excessive inebriation. The motto of reformers was, "A self-governing nation must be inhabited by self-governing individuals." The first public health movement in this country was the temperance movement. Despite the lack of sophisticated communications, per capita consumption of liquor fell by half in a little more than a decade.

The 1830s saw the rise of what historians call the Second Great Awakening of renewed religious fervor. The abolition movement against slavery was a direct result of the Second Great Awakening.

Williams' book is well-timed. A few years ago his message would have fallen on hostile or indifferent ears. The mood is now changing. The U.S. is at the dawn of a series of reform movements—spiritual, social, political, economic. Williams' volume will be a clarion catalyst for this reawakening.

Preface

They snatched me off the basketball court. They sprayed a whole lot of Mace in my face, put a gun to my head, and took me to the car, and took me to Potomac Gardens, the projects. They were trying to get some money from my buddy. They kept saying that they wanted a half a ki' or $20,000.

They didn't get, but they snatched me up. They were trying to put that tape and stuff on my legs. All that Mace was really burning me up. I jumped out the car over near the projects. They shot at me about ten times. I ran up Pennsylvania Avenue, and I got hit by a car. Next thing I knew I was in the hospital over at D.C. General.

Meet Brad Howard. At twenty-nine he has already exceeded his life expectancy. Many of his closest friends are dead. He spent all of his adult life, and most of his teenage years, as a street hustler in southeast Washington, D.C. Liberal politicians would call him a "troubled black youth." To most white conservatives, he would be known as a member of the "criminal class." But in fact, as you will see, Brad does not fit either stereotype.

I met Brad a year ago during a speech at the Greater Southeast Hospital Complex in Washington, D.C. At the time I was hosting a nightly radio program in Washington, and he had listened to my show. I often speak on my program about the need for young men like Brad to stop making excuses, to take responsibility for their lives, and to meet their obligations. The message is simple and uncompromising. In response I frequently get lambasted by my callers. The better-educated listeners usually complain that I do not understand the plight of inner-city youth, while the less educated call to spin their elaborate theories of white conspiracy. In the eyes of both groups I have earned the label "black conservative"—a pejorative rather than descriptive term.

As is my usual practice when young people call me, I arranged to meet with Brad and discuss his situation. Most of the young people who call never show up. Brad actually did. As we talked, I began to realize that something about his appeal was unusually genuine, as if the conscience that lay dormant in him for more than a decade had begun to stir.

Brad represents the sort of personalized challenge politicians and commentators fear. People in my business, liberal and conservative, find it easy to confront Brad's problems from a distance, and from behind the protective shield of a microphone or a newspaper column. We view his situation through the telescope of statistics on poverty, illegitimacy, and education. We have made into an art form the ability to describe, deconstruct, and solve his problems in seven hundred words, less if the *Washington Post* is short on space.

During our conversation, I thought of my liberal friends who earn paychecks by writing empathetic editorials about "inner-city youths." If only we would repeal the

Reagan welfare cuts, they argue, Brad's problems would be solved. Having thus solved the problems of the "inner city," they make their nightly pilgrimage to a comfortable place in well-defended suburban enclaves on the Potomac, where they can bask in the warmth of a deed well done. It is, I have always thought, a singularly sensible hypocrisy.

I also thought of my conservative friends, people ready to assure anyone who will listen that their policies will "liberate" Brad and others like him from the dependency and defeatism of welfare. If only we would repeal Johnson's Great Society programs, say, replacing "welfare" with "workfare," Brad's problems will be solved. Having thus solved the problems created by the welfare state, they join their liberal neighbors on the banks of the Potomac.

And so as darkness descends, liberals and conservatives alike gather to reassure one another that the defamatory comments made on "Nightline" were nothing personal. And then, while cocktails are served, the discussion turns to the issue of which think tank is in the ascendancy.

It is not that either group lacks genuine concern, but Brad's problems seem intractable. Increasingly, policy "experts" believe that the social breakdown Brad represents may be unsolvable. Thankfully, it is a belief Brad does not share.

In time I was able to place Brad in an office job here in Washington, where he continues his struggle to break free of his old life and make good on his vow to change. But in speaking with him I began to wonder how he might view my own philosophy and what, if anything, it could offer him. This book seeks to answer that question.

It begins with Brad's story, told from his point of view. This chapter is a composite of five interviews I had with him over several weeks last year. The facts about Brad's life are true—at least insofar as he was honest—but several key details, including his name, have been changed to help conceal his identity. The seven brief essays that follow are written as letters to Brad. They are intended, however, for a much broader audience. After all, Brad had many accomplices as he chose the New Jack lifestyle, including many of those people gathered at the cocktail party on the Potomac. I hope they recognize themselves in these essays. I am certain Brad will.

Acknowledgments

I owe a great debt of gratitude to all those who helped make this book possible, for their exemplary patience, diligence, and expertise. I would especially like to thank my staff at Graham Williams Group for their invaluable contributions: Tracy Hymes for her many hours with Brad, striving to come to a deeper understanding of the forces at work in his life; Tangela Parks and Akili West, for their thoughtful suggestions as they labored over the various changes in the manuscript; and Steve Schwalm, whose writing and editing skills throughout the project helped bring to life my voice and my views.

I also must thank Griff Jenkins, Stedman Graham, Mike Lewis, Robert Cooper, and Paul and Ira Hersh for their indispensable support and assistance, and my brothers Alvin, Kent, Gerald, and Bruce and sisters Mary Williams and Mary Boyd, who share in my spirit as well as my blood.

I also owe an overwhelming debt to Adam Bellow and David Bernstein at the Free Press, who believed in this project from the beginning and whose perseverance and vision helped bring its seeds to fruition.

Finally, I must thank Brad, who will necessarily remain anonymous, for hearing and responding to my message, for sharing with me his views and experiences, and especially for having the courage to take it upon himself to try and make the changes that he saw were necessary.

Chapter One

"I Had a Lot of Power"

When middle-class Americans think of black street hustlers, they usually imagine the movie images of New Jack City. Hollywood's latest version of street hustlers portrays them as clever, calculating young men who use their considerable talent to run organized crime. These new films paint hustlers as handsome rogues with Errol Flynn appeal and always with a beautiful, refined woman. It is as if Hollywood decided not to take the trouble to create a new character and simply slapped a black face on the Godfather. The alternative type has Hollywood hustlers tending to be hapless victims of circumstance, usually the pawn of some white (or Hispanic) drug lord who uses threats and coercion to force them to do his evil deeds. In both cases, street hustlers are depicted as personally compelling, and often sympathetic, characters. The reality is different from both types, neither glamorous nor melodramatic.

During the 1980s Brad Howard, now twenty-nine years old, made his living as a sort of street corner drug lord, selling powdered cocaine, crack, PCP, and heroin in Washington, D.C. At the apex of his career, Brad raked in more than $200,000 a year. He owned a Mercedes-Benz and an upscale townhouse, dressed in expensive clothes, and took lavish vacations. For his amusement Brad assembled a harem of women who shared his bed in exchange for drugs, jewelry, clothes, expensive meals, and other trinkets. He slept with an automatic weapon at his side and tucked a semiautomatic pistol in his belt whenever he left the house.

But unlike the New Jack movie hustler, the women Brad knew were more likely to be hard-up drug addicts or cast-off teenagers than sophisticated beauties. As is typical of most other street hustlers, even when he was rich, Brad lived more like the characters of *Do the Right Thing* than *The Great Gatsby*—the main difference from the former being that Brad took his Mercedes through the McDonalds drive-through rather than walked into the store. And also like most other street hustlers, Brad is not some unappreciated criminal genius but rather a misguided inventory clerk. He is a C minus student with a lousy education and little motivation. He adopted the street hustler life because it was easy, because it was something he could learn quickly, and, most of all, because nobody ever tried to stop him.

If Brad is far from the Godfather stereotype of New Jack City, he is even further from Hollywood's version of the hapless black victim pushed into hustling by poverty and circumstance. During our first interview, I expected to hear Brad tell the familiar story of being raised in a poor single-parent home in the inner city. Instead Brad admitted, "I had a good father, a good mother. My mother worked at the Department of Agriculture. My father worked at the Capitol, doing printing. He always used to work, take us to work with him. We used to be together a lot. Me and my father, all of us are real close." As it turns out, Brad is one of the increasingly rare young black men who came from an intact, working-class family. His parents and his older brothers are what used to be called good, honest folk. Ironically, his oldest brother makes his living as a correction officer in New York State, where he spends his nights watching over young criminals like Brad. The second brother works for a trucking company. Both are married and have successful families of their own. Tragically the same cannot be said for Brad's younger brother, who followed him into the hustling lifestyle and is now in prison serving a seven-year sentence for delivering the drugs Brad gave him.

As he told his story I began to view Brad as more like a spoiled middle-class teenager than a ghetto hustler. This assumption did not last long either. When he began spending time on the streets, as Brad puts it, his parents "came down on me real hard." Brad's mother was deeply religious, and until he was in his teens Brad sang in the church choir and regularly attended Sunday school. She would warn Brad that "he was doin' no good out there on the streets" and advise him "to read the Bible more." Brad's father, for his part, didn't mince words. One afternoon he announced: "You know I'm buying a [burial] plot for you and your brother." As Brad recounts the story, "I said, 'So you're already counting on our death?' And my father said, 'You won't stop running the streets like you running.' Yep. Just think, how many people's fathers say that to them?"

Brad's parents clearly did not fit the stereotype of disengaged urban black parents who let their children run wild. They had raised all of their children to go to church, showed them to live the right way, and set a good example themselves. Nor did his parents seem anything like the overly permissive upper-class liberals whose children so often go wrong. Clearly they believed they were doing their best to set and enforce limits on their teenage son. When they found out that Brad was dealing, for example, his parents warned him not to bring drugs into their house and repeatedly told him he was doing the wrong thing. As Brad talked, it became clear that this was the limit of what he and his parents meant by "coming down real hard" on him—and I got my first true glimpse into the mind-set that has guided his life.

The way Brad's mother and father responded to their son's criminality represents a view that I have since discovered is fairly common among urban parents: they feel as though most of what their children do is beyond their control. While many middle-class parents—both black and white—would have called the police or thrown out their teenage son if he became a crack dealer, Brad's parents continued to provide him with his $200 monthly allowance and meekly voice their displeasure. At some level, both Brad and his parents believed that drug dealing was unacceptable but also that it was a fairly normal occupation for a teenager. They reacted to Brad's career choice in much the same way a suburban parent might react to a daughter's posing in *Penthouse:* they strongly disapproved but viewed it as his choice to make.

I have contrasted Brad and his parents with middle-class

families several times, but in truth Brad's is a middle-class family. That, as much as any of his crimes, is what makes his story so disturbing. Although he grew up mostly in Southeast Washington, an area with a reputation for being dangerous and crime-infested, he and his family lived on a quiet street in a working-class neighborhood. His parents have a good income and live a comfortable life. In fact, Brad even finished high school. So, in fact, it is incorrect to describe Brad and his family as "underprivileged," or "from the inner city," or "part of the underclass." Instead, I call Brad a "street hustler" who lives in the "ghetto." I will explain a bit later why I think these are the most accurate labels, but before I do I should let Brad describe how he entered this life in his own words:

> When I was, like, in the tenth grade, one of my friends, he was into hustling, selling drugs, and I didn't really know about it. He was like, go give this to Stevie or something. They called it boat, lovely, PCP, reefa. I used to go give it to him. Sometimes I used to go with him to Fourteenth and U Streets; they were selling heroin, dope. One day I sat up there the whole day, they made about fifteen thousand. I guess I just got involved.
>
> I was like nineteen or twenty, I had a 190E Mercedes-Benz. I was like paying $500, almost $600 car notes. I ain't care. I had some of everything. I had a Maxima, a MPV [mini] van. I got so much money I did everything a rich person could do. What couldn't I do? We were young—twenty-three, twenty-four, going to Las Vegas, went to Hawaii, water skiing, scuba diving, and I didn't even know how to swim.

In just two paragraphs Brad refuted all of the sociolo-
gists, psychologists, and politicians who have made careers
out of trying to explain why young black men turn to
crime. For Brad and for every other hustler he knew, it was
simple greed. Even today when asked about his days as a
hustler, he thinks first of the money he made and boasts of
the things he was able to buy. It was all great fun to him
and his friends, and the fact they they derived their wealth
from selling poison to poor black people seemed to make
no difference to any of them. Brad the Godfather? Hardly.
It was more like a decade-long "Animal House."

Just as Brad was not the Godfather, his gang was anything but the mafia. Like most other hustlers, nearly as
soon as Brad began selling drugs, he also got the gang religion. With his "little crew," Brad enforced dominance over
his turf and proved his manhood—such as it was. This was
not the well-orchestrated crime ring of Hollywood fame,
and Brad was not a prisoner of his past life. In the movies,
gang members are bound for life and face death if they
leave. In Brad's world, gang members are temporary associates, and the only thing that kept him on the streets was
his greed. All of this suited Brad just fine for awhile, but
then he started getting scared:

> I was real comfortable, I was real happy. I kept saying I was
> going to stop, I was going to work. I didn't want to die out
> on the streets selling drugs, or I didn't want to be incarcer-
> ated for fifteen or twenty years. I wanted to work; it just
> seemed like I got deeper into it, deeper into it. Instead of
> me trying to better myself by work ing, I just got deeper

into it. I would get in so deep I was staying out all night and I was coming out two o'clock in the morning hustling.

Have a little crew, you know; they called it a gang, you know. And we were terrorizing people. I never was the killing type. In my whole life I shot three people. I ain't care. I don't know if they died or didn't die. I didn't care.

I have been through like drive by's and all that. I did it all. I had a lot of people looking out for me. I had guys do, like, I could say, 'I don't like him, man, kill him. I just give you what you want, just kill him. I give you five, I give you a thousand, just kill him. I give it to you now.' They'd go get the pistol, whatever. They'd get him up out of there.

To say that Brad was a cold-blooded killer is an astonishing understatement. Murder was so casual to him that even now he does not consider himself the "killing type" because he personally shot only three people (though he did not wait around long enough to see if they were dead). Brad used violence as a business tool to undercut the competition, protect his market share, or gain goodwill. The only time violence had any sort of lasting impact on Brad was when he himself was the victim of a kidnapping. Dragged off a basketball court in D.C., sprayed with Mace, and violently threatened at gunpoint, Brad barely escaped by running into traffic. Dodging bullets, he wasn't quite able to dodge an oncoming car.

This incident had a profound effect on Brad. In an

instant, all the phony courage and bravado vanished as Brad feared for his life. Today, when asked why he stopped hustling, Brad comes straight to the point:

> What really scared me to stop completely was the guys that kidnapped me. They just snatched me off the basketball court. I'm changing my life. I'm changing my life because I've been through a lot. I mean, I got kidnapped before, almost got killed; I got shot at a couple times. I just ain't with it. I ain't with none of that no more. I mean, I'm living a life.

There it is. The incident that changed Brad's life was that he himself was finally the victim of his own criminality. He has no remorse, no guilt, no recognition of the damage he has done to others. In a perverse modern version of Saint Paul's experience on the road to Damascus, the scales fell from Brad's eyes: "I mean . . . I almost got killed."

Earlier in his career there were two other opportunities for Brad to have a similar experience. The police, aware for some time of his drug trafficking, had tried to set traps to catch him. Twice Brad was arrested, and the second time he sat in jail for two months awaiting trial on felony drug charges. Again his parents came to his rescue, this time using their house and car as collateral to bail him out of jail. During the year Brad spent awaiting trial, the judge placed him under house arrest using an electronic device attached to his ankle to keep him close to home. But the electronic gadget did little to discourage Brad from plying his trade; within a few months he again began dealing drugs, now directly from his parents' house. Sometimes he would leave the house for a few hours to get or sell drugs, returning in time to check in with the telephone and the electronic device on his ankle.

Brad, staring at a sentence of thirty to sixty years in prison for violating federal drug trafficking laws, used his drug money and the help of his parents to hire a good lawyer. He was able to beat the charge. The judge, Brad explains, looked favorably on his story to such an extent that even Brad is surprised that he got off. Obviously, the judge thought that Brad was just another young man who inadvertently ended up on the wrong end of the system— probably for lack of real opportunity. In a sense, you can't blame the judge. Brad did not have a criminal record as an adult, since his youthful encounters with the law were hidden from the legal system under rules that prevent juvenile criminal history from being reopened once the person turns eighteen. The judge was also swayed by several women who went to church with Brad and his mother and who testified that he was a good kid.

After the trial was over, Brad returned to the streets. In fact, he had been dealing drugs all through his time awaiting trial and during the trial itself. Ironically, the legal system found him not guilty of drug trafficking.

If this trial taught Brad any lesson, it was that the legal system is largely incapable of dealing with young hustlers. While the prospect of incarceration was real, and unappealing, to him, Brad also knew his chances of being caught, much less convicted, were small. On a deeper level, the legal system reinforced Brad's view that people are not held accountable for their actions and that the entire system was constructed to help people like him explain away their past. It was not until his younger brother was sentenced to jail and Brad was kidnapped that this attitude began to change.

More than the legal system reinforced Brad's belief that he would not be held accountable for his actions. Throughout life Brad has approached relationships with women as casually as most people interact with pets. This is not to say that Brad fits the image of the rap-singing misogynist. In fact, when I asked him about that image, he replied, "I don't listen to rap music. I don't like it." Rather, Brad's views toward women are better described as those of a superradicalized male feminist. He has absolutely no doubt that women are as capable as men, and he lives that view. Whether in business dealings or sex, Brad almost never even thinks about treating "females," as he calls them, any differently than he does men—with little concern and no respect. If women have sex with him, that is their choice and their responsibility. If they want to buy drugs from him, they have to pay just as any man would. Indeed, the only difference in Brad's eyes is that women possess a commodity that he values: a woman's anatomy. But even this does not cause Brad to think differently of women. Instead, he appreciates their ability to trade this commodity in the same way he would appreciate any man's ability to trade money or drugs or guns. But he also resents them for being able to exact payment of one kind or another in exchange for sex. In this respect Brad thinks of women the way I think of the post office: I have to deal with it because it is the only game in town, but I don't trust it and I don't like it.

I don't trust no females. Just my mother. I don't really trust my girlfriend. I spent so much money on females, I don't even know how much I spent. I go blow about $4,000 on different females, take them shopping. You can verify with any of my friends, I probably been with fifteen hundred different women in my life. I had a lot of power.

Even this characterization fails to capture Brad's attitudes toward women completely, because, like most other young black men, his views are shaped by two opposing forces: the women he used for sex and the women his mother's age. Brad claims to respect older women, but scratch the surface, and that respect too amounts to nothing more than his recognition that they possess a commodity he values: standing in the community. Early on, Brad learned that this standing could be useful to him. When I asked him specifically why he respected the women his mother knows, he said, "They were always behind me when I went to court and like that." As the judge in his trial had taught him, these women and the standing they enjoy can be valuable indeed to a street hustler trying to beat a drug rap.

Throughout his hustling, Brad did settle into a steady relationship with one woman, although having a girlfriend did little to curb his sexual appetite, and he maintained regular sexual relationships with his harem. Still, this woman did provide him something of an anchor and the only tenuous connection to life outside himself. In 1988 Brad's girlfriend gave birth to the first of their three daughters. As with his encounter with the courts, this experience had the potential to change his attitude about hustling and his lifestyle. He even tried to quit hustling, but again no one demanded that he stop hustling or even care for his children.

As he told me the story of his first child's birth, I was in for the biggest shock of all. I had expected Brad to be the violent, self-centered thug he revealed to me, but even I was not prepared for this: "When my first child was born I was working for [a Washington trade association]. I was real happy and I was, like, I'm a stop doing what I'm doing." But before long, his late-night hustling left him too tired to make it to work, "So I just quitted." "You were working?" I asked incredulously. "Yeah, I've had a lot of jobs. I was never fired from any of 'em, I just quitted."

This blasted the final myth I had assumed about Brad: that he was compelled to become a hustler because he did not have, or at least did not know about, the job opportunities that could have lifted him off the streets. He had found and rejected many times the path his older brothers had taken. Neither his encounter with the courts nor the birth of his first child, and not even the destruction he could see himself leaving in his wake, were enough to compel him to choose that path. Not that Brad thinks there is anything wrong with being a hard-working citizen, mind you; he just takes the I'm okay–you're okay attitude to an extreme. Unfortunately, so does the culture around him, and for years it has reinforced the idea that Brad was okay just as he was.

But even Brad's self-centered, detached views and destructive lifestyle could not completely extinguish his instinctive concern for his children. Although personal fear remains the chief factor motivating his retreat from the streets, his children's welfare continues to be an important part of Brad's desire to start a new life:

> I be trying to think back on all the stuff I did, and I be trying to think, like, into the future. Like what am I gonna have in five, six years? What I'm be doing? Because I can't go to jail and leave my kids suffering. I try to look all around, and I say I can't go out on my kids like that. I can't set an example for my kids like that. I can't die or go to jail. I gotta be there for my kids. If I go back on the street, I'm gonna get killed. I already know it. I want my kids to be there with a father.

I was thrilled by Brad's concern and thought that I had finally found some common ground with this young man. Brad was not much like the usual portrait of the deadbeat dad so reviled and vilified in the media. But I was wrong. In Brad's world, the notion of what it means to be a good father assumes a narrow, peculiar definition. By this, he does not mean staying at home, or even coming home most nights, to help raise his daughters. Nor does he mean that he should take responsibility for their actions. In his view, being a good father does not even extend to worrying about his children's schooling. Instead it means providing his girlfriend with enough money to meet her bills. So when he speaks of his time on the streets, Brad is quick to point out that he was once a good father: "The way I was living at one point, I was real comfortable. I did used to do for [his girlfriend and his daughters], and I was twenty-one. I provided for my kids." Although he has never married the woman he usually calls "the mother of my daughters," Brad notes with some conviction that he and his girlfriend are "real close" and see each other "mostly every day."

Ironically, with his daughters now ranging in age from four to six, Brad has taken it upon himself to teach his girls about the dangers of drugs. "They see a little bag or something laying on the ground or anywhere, they walk around it. They might say, 'That's crack, Ma.' You know. It ain't got to be nothing in it, but they know." With paternal pride he adds, "They real smart." This drug education is clearly beyond the call of duty for someone who views fatherhood as Brad does, but he is willing to go the extra mile.

Given that Brad does not quite fit any of the usual stereotypes when it comes to violence, or fatherhood, or women, or even drugs, it did not surprise me that he takes an unusual view of race as well. The Spike Lee version of Brad would have a deep-seated race consciousness, his situation would be clearly linked in some important way to the fact that he is black, and he would have a deep animosity toward people of other races. But on issue of race, Brad oscillates between a casual acceptance of different races and a unique version of black pride:

> As far as now, I don't really care for white people too much. I won't say all white people. I got a good friend, he white. I had a friend named Anita. I used to go with her about two years. She became a police officer. Like if I see her today, she don't even speak. She work up in Georgetown now. She act like the other race. She act like she white now.

When I asked him whether he had encountered much racism, Brad's thoughts turned to several specific instances in which white people had treated him badly. He first recalled that people with whom he used to work made disparaging comments behind his back. "They smile at you, but it's times I know I walk past and they say little slick stuff out their mouth." He also told a story of six white men calling him "nigger" and threatening him in Georgetown. Then Brad described a situation in which he was walking on the sidewalk when a woman bumped into him. Instead of saying "excuse me" she said, "Shit." Brad viewed this as a clear sign of disrespect, but he let it go. A moment later he added, "I ain't saying it's all whites. Like two years ago, I'd have killed them. Now I won't go like that." Like many of the younger African Americans I know, Brad seems unable to distinguish between true racism and the kind of personal tensions everyone encounters every day.

Unlike some middle-class blacks whom I know, Brad does not let racist incidents, real or imagined, rule his life. He just does not think about race much, and he generally takes a pragmatic view. He accepts as a matter of faith the idea that there are two disparate cultures in America, one black and one white. He believes that these cultural differences, from ways of dress to manners of speech, represent obstacles to blacks when they are trying to get jobs, but he doesn't dwell on those obstacles. As Brad has calculated it, a person in the white world should obey the local customs, "talk proper like," and the same is true when a white person comes into his world. Brad sees the universe as comprising two different worlds, one "black," one "white," each with its own set of values, each with its own accepted ways of acting and thinking. I asked him about that, and he just smiled and said, "Oh, you know, some black people, they be actin' one way, you know, when they made it. I ain't sayin' they not black or nothin'. It don't matter to me. I'm, like, you want to be that way, that's fine. I have no problem with it. You know."

After five interviews with Brad I had begun to wonder what, if anything, I could say that might help him. To be honest, I wondered why I should even try. I had in front of me an unrepentant murderer who got rich selling drugs to the poor. But I had in front of me as well the future of black America. If I could help Brad to shatter his old assumptions about the world and break out of his personal ghetto, I would be helping his three daughters. Beneath all of his cockiness, I sensed a genuine concern for those little girls, and even if it was misguided, it could serve as a start. More than that, I could not bring myself to consider the alternative, which is to do nothing. I could not in good conscience send this hustler back to the streets without trying to change him.

The fact that someone like Brad, who had all the advantages of a stable, loving, middle-class home, could fall prey to the lure of the ghetto ethic has grim implications for the next generation of African Americans. Beyond the stereotyping by both liberals and conservatives, here was a living and breathing example of the worst pathologies facing America. Concerned men and women must, I firmly believe, come to understand the allure that the streets hold for so many of our teenagers—the poor and vulnerable as much as the affluent and secure. In a sense my work with Brad was an experiment to see whether by engaging with him one on one, man to man, I could help him recover some portion of the humanity he lost on the streets.

I use the term *street hustler* to describe Brad and the people like him, drawing on a phrase Malcolm X coined. To be more specific, Malcolm used the term *ghetto hustler* to describe people like Brad. The term *ghetto* is rarely used these days, mostly because it is associated with an earlier era in the civil rights struggle. Nonetheless, I think it is appropriate.

The word *ghetto* was first used to describe the rundown areas where Jews were segregated in Europe. In postwar America "the ghetto" referred to the predominantly black slums in most major cities, and it later became synonymous with all manner of cultural pathologies before it disappeared from popular discourse. Brad clearly did not grow up in a geographic region that could properly be called a ghetto, but he has just as clearly adopted the worst values that term conveys. In his mind's eye, Brad and his friends are just as much residents of the ghetto as Malcolm was in his days as a hustler. The fact that he is black is almost incidental; I have met plenty of white people who adopted the same sort of ghetto mentality, but they were known, at least where I grew up in South Carolina, as "white trash." Young African Americans seem particularly vulnerable to the call of this new ghetto. Brad's attitudes about everything from other human beings to himself leave little doubt that he is a true citizen of this realm.

Still, I should admit that I am using the term *ghetto hustler* with some hesitation. It is all too certain that our society is creating new Brads at a disturbing rate, and it is equally certain that this destructive subculture is increasingly finding new adherents in middle-class black families like Brad's. There is good reason to worry. These hustlers are, after all, people so terrifying that Malcolm X remarked, "It scared me the first time I really saw the danger of these ghetto teenagers if they are ever sparked to violence." Their presence is even more disturbing because they are not necessarily the product of rundown neighborhoods, lousy schools, or any of the other external factors that once characterized the ghetto. Instead, they are the product of a philosophy that is aggressively promoted in almost every corner of black America. Unlike the old ghettos of the sixties, there is no amount of money that can rebuild or revitalize the ghetto in which Brad operates; it can be repaired only by helping Brad to reclaim his humanity and learn to appreciate the humanity of others. No series of letters would be sufficient for this task, but I hope these are a beginning.

Chapter Two

"I Was Never the Killin' Type"

Dear Brad:

Since our first telephone conversation, I have been thinking about your situation and what I can do to help you succeed. When you asked me to help you start a new life, I was confident that as long as you really wanted to make a decent life for yourself and your family, I could help you. Of course, I did not really know you then, but I thought I knew your type. I assumed you were one of those young black men I have heard about so often—young men who turn to selling drugs because they see no other good alternative. I thought that all you really needed was some guidance—what might be called a mentor—and a decent opportunity to prove yourself.

It is ironic that I would make all of these assumptions. After all, I am best known for being a black "conservative," yet these are the assumptions of political "liberals," who believe that the pervasive racism in America forces people like you to turn to crime because you have no other opportunities. I have always rejected that idea. Since I have become a successful businessman despite this racism, I thought I could help you do the same. But in the back of my mind, I shared many of the same assumptions that my liberal friends have. I too believed that the reason many young black men turn to crime is that they do not see other opportunities. The main difference between my views and those of liberals was that I recognize that plenty of opportunities exist. I also believed that the self-defeating ideology of many black leaders prevents young men like you from learning how to take advantage of them. I was confident I could help you because, I reasoned, the only thing standing between you and a decent life is your inability to see the opportunities around you. Not that I believed your transition from the streets would be an easy one, but I was pretty sure I knew how to begin. Now I am not so sure.

As I listened to your story, I kept thinking of something Malcolm X wrote in his autobiography: "The most dangerous black man in America is the street hustler." "The ghetto hustler," he continued, "is internally restrained by nothing. He has no religion, no concept of morality, no civic responsibility, no fear—nothing . . . He is constantly preying upon others, probing for any human weakness like a ferret."

I am sorry to say it, but in many respects you remind me of the street hustler Malcolm described. The problem you face has virtually nothing to do with a lack of opportunities; you have had a slew of them. No, Brad, the problem you face is to remake your outlook on life completely. Somehow you must go from being the most dangerous black man in America to a moral, responsible, self-respecting human being. To make matters worse, you do not even realize what you have become.

As I thought about your problem, I began wishing that my liberal friends were right. If you were just another poor black victim of racism, then solutions would be easy. I could point you in the direction of the people, agencies, and institutions designed to give you a second chance and then help you work through the difficulties of the bureaucracy. I know some people would think that I am exaggerating the help the system now offers to people like you, but I do not think I am. Imagine what it would have been like to hold out to the poor black men and women of my grandfather's generation, people who scratched out a living by working as farm hands in the racist, rural South, what I can offer to you. Here you are, a young black man with a criminal record, a lousy education, and no real experience, and I know plenty of people who would give you a second chance at a job and a career, a second chance at an education, even a second chance at building a reputation. Even now I can say with confidence that you can go as far in America as your abilities will take you. You may not realize it, but the whole American system is structured to give people like you a second, third, and even a fourth chance.

I imagine myself standing in front of those sharecroppers of two generations past and telling them the same thing. Need an education? No problem. I can hook you up at a community college. Need a job? No problem. I can help you find plenty of them. Need help for your family? No problem. When you start working, you will be eligible for payments direct from the government that will more than replace any money you lose by leaving welfare. The system will even help you pay for medical care for your children and cover almost all the costs of your education (for the second time). Need to prove yourself? No problem. Just show me that you are willing to lead a clean life, and I, or almost any of the people I know, will personally go to bat for you.

Those old farm hands would think I had gone crazy.

Now, Brad, I am not saying that the opportunities I can offer will transport you effortlessly to Easy Street; you will have to work hard day and night to take advantage of them. You will struggle financially, living from paycheck to paycheck until you prove yourself in the workplace. Often you will feel as though you are set back one step each time you take two steps forward. But compared to the kind of hard work my parents and grandparents did, you will have it easy. Even as you are starting out, you will be economically far better off than most African Americans of my grandparents' generation ever were. It won't be easy, but the opportunities are there, and once you seize them it will only get better.

It all seemed so easy after our first conversation when all I thought you needed were some new opportunities. Now that I have come to know you, I realize that what you really need is a new soul—or at least some serious repair work on the one you have. Aside from your children, you seem to care for no one but yourself. I wish you could have sat in my chair and listened to yourself. Throughout our conversations, you never once expressed regret for all the people you hurt. You never once mentioned the drug addicts whose lives you helped to destroy. You never even talked about how you betrayed your parents. Instead you just shook your head, smiled, and said, "Dag, I did all that." Is that really all it meant to you? As you think about the people you shot or the addicts whose habit you served, do you ever think about their children? These are the fathers who will never come home because you ordered them killed. These are the mothers whose children are dying of AIDS because they could not afford to pay your price for a clean needle to inject the heroin you sold them. You are the creator of crack babies, fatherless children, and the criminal class that plagues poor black neighborhoods. While Jesse Jackson chanted "Keep Hope Alive," you were busy working to destroy it. And for what? A Hawaiian vacation?

When you were on the streets, you became the worst kind of predator: you became a cannibal, killing your own kind so you could live well. You paid for your trips to Las Vegas by selling heroin to black people so desperate for drugs that they sold their children's food stamps to pay you. You made your car payments by selling crack to young black women so desperate for another rock that they prostituted their bodies so they could pay your price. The toys you bought for your children were paid for with the blood of the black men you killed, or had killed, to protect your turf. Those are not the facts as I see them; they are the facts as you have told them to me. While you dropped $5,000 on the blackjack tables, some child just like your sweet daughters was going to bed hungry so her mother or father could give you money for drugs. You did all of this as casually as most people squash a cockroach. To you the lives of these people meant nothing more than that. You used drugs to build your ghetto Roach Motel where black teenagers "check in but they don't check out."

Even as I write this, I can feel you welling up with pride. If your soul was not all but destroyed, you would feel remorse and shame, but knowing you as I now do, I suspect you are thinking again of that phrase you used: "I had a lot of power." Well, Brad, so did the plantation overseers during the days of slavery. That is what you have become: an overseer of young African Americans working your ghetto plantation for yourself and for the people who sold you drugs. Instead of a whip you carried a gun. During your turf battles, you and other dealers traded ownership of drug addicts just as callously as the auctioneer sold our ancestors. But by using drug addiction instead of shackles to keep your slaves in check, you have accomplished something no slave owner ever could: you bought and sold souls. Remember this the next time you look back fondly on your life on the street: each year in Washington, D.C., more black people are murdered by black criminals than were killed in all of the Ku Klux Klan lynchings of this century. People like you, Brad, are more dangerous to our community than the Klan.

I too have walked the streets of Southeast Washington, and I have seen your handiwork. I have seen the crack addicts huddled on heating grates in the winter and sorting through the garbage outside my office for something to eat. I have seen the young black women trying to sell their bodies for sex while their small children looked on just so they could pay for another vial. I have seen the young boys admiring the expensive cars of young hustlers like you and hoping one day to follow in your path. It is little wonder that people often call my radio program to say that drugs are part of a broad conspiracy against our race. But you and I know different. The reason the street hustler takes to the streets is greed. The streets do not "get hold" of him; he sets out to conquer the 'hood. New cars, nice clothes, and free sex are worth more to him than the lives of other human beings. The street hustler betrays his race and his humanity for trinkets. In time, he can no longer tell the difference between right and wrong; he literally sells his soul for a few years of the good life.

Even so, a conscience is hard to kill. So the street hustler develops a sort of personal ethical code that helps to quiet his occasional feelings of guilt. That is what happened to you, Brad. You speak with pride of your policy not to sell drugs to women you know, as if the women you do not know were any less human. You make yourself feel better by claiming "I was never the killing type" because you did not personally pull the trigger—at least not very often. Well, Brad, you may not have pulled the trigger, but you paid others to do it for you. And while your 9 mm is probably more efficient, the needles you sold are just as effective at killing people in the long run.

Brad, you were definitely the killing type.

Now you have come to ask for my help. You, who still do not believe you were the "killing type," say you are ready to change. I believe you are ready to change, but as you said, "I'm changing my life because I've been through a lot. I mean I got kidnapped before, almost got killed. I got shot at a couple of times." That is like an overseer's quitting his job because he got scared after the Nat Turner rebellion. He may stop working with slaves, but he is still just a vile, brutal, soulless man. You can begin changing your life only when you start to realize what you have done.

I am reminded of something Eldridge Cleaver wrote in his book, *Soul on Ice*. Eldridge was a hustler like you, but he was also a rapist, and when he was finally put in prison it was for committing several rapes. His book was seen by most people as an explanation of the political and social forces that compel young black men to turn to crime. But it was also clear that Eldridge had reflected in the book the first steps in a very personal journey that would help him recapture his soul. After being caught Eldridge writes, "I took a long look at myself and, for the first time in my life, admitted that I was wrong, that I had gone astray. . . . Even thought I had some insight into my own motivations, I did not feel justified. I lost my self-respect. My pride as a man dissolved and my whole fragile moral structure seemed to collapse, completely shattered."

Brad, you seem to be at this stage in your life, with your self-respect and your moral structure unshaken. I doubt that you can make any real progress away from the streets unless that changes. But I am also concerned about a more practical problem you will face. As you try to leave the streets, I do not think you will get much encouragement from the people around you. From the young women who used to admire your material wealth and tried to curry your favor, to the young children who treated you with a dignity you did not deserve, your new life will bring more criticism than praise. You will be tempted to counter their jeers by reciting your record of crime, just as you did with me. If you yield to that temptation, you are already on the road back into your former life. Every time you boast of the things you used to have—your money, your guns, and your women—you are moving closer to the streets.

It is time you recognized that your self-serving view has been constantly reinforced by your community. The media like to call what you were doing "black-on-black crime." I suppose the phrase makes white suburbanites feel safer. It certainly allows them to believe it is not really their problem. Personally, I have always hated the phrase. When people say "black-on-black crime," the victim somehow seems less important, even partly to blame. It also makes the criminal feel as though what he is doing is somehow natural, maybe expected. Even many leading black political leaders encourage your views by speaking of black criminals as though they were the fault and responsibility of the African Americans. There is no doubt that if white teenagers were being gunned down at such an alarming rate, we would not have the same sort of clinical detachment permitted by the cliché "black-on-black."

Then there are the adults within your community— your own parents and their friends, and the others too. I do not like to criticize your parents, but think of why you respect the women of your mother's generation. You said it was because "they stood behind me" when you were in court. This protective instinct among many black women is uniquely strong, but it is equally misguided. These women would rather side with you, an admitted drug dealer and probably a murderer, than accept the idea that one of their own may belong in prison. This unconditional acceptance is crucial to most street hustlers. It props up the image they have of themselves as decent people, even if they know some of what they are doing is wrong. The fact that you say you "respect" the women who give you that kind of support shows me that you are still not far from the streets. If you genuinely understood what you had done, you would respect the women who cursed you and hid their children from you, not the women who coddled and protected you.

So, Brad, it is time for you to confront that part of your life you hide beneath stories of wealth and success. I want you to go with me to tour Southeast Washington and see your legacy. I want you to spend an evening in the emergency room of D.C. General looking at the faces of the boys brought in there on stretchers each day. I want you to meet one of the mothers whose child was lost to your drugs and one of the children whose father was lost to the streets. I hope that, like Eldridge Cleaver, you will find relief in accepting responsibility for what you have done. But even if you find no relief, you may find your conscience, which is something you will need if you intend to change your life.

I should also tell you honestly, Brad, that if you do not accept this invitation, you cannot expect any help from me. Instead, I will take the transcripts of our conversations to the police, and I will do whatever I can to see to it that you are never again able to destroy so many lives. I will not stand by as you reinstitute slavery on the streets of my city, and if that means betraying our trust, I will.

I hope you will choose to do the right thing.

Sincerely,

Armstrong

Chapter Three

"I Feel Good to Be a Black Male"

Dear Brad:

When we first met, you said you regretted your life as a street hustler and that you would make different choices if you could live your live over again. When I asked why you stopped hustling, you explained, "What really made me stop was the guys who kidnapped me." I guess I should be shocked at your reaction, but I am not. It was not until hustling became too dangerous for you that you stopped. You do not regret having used women; you are only sorry that you risked getting AIDS. Even when you talk of providing for your children, you seem to be motivated mostly by the fact that you are embarrassed. That is why I was so convinced that you were completely sincere when you said you wished to start a new life: you had decided that hustling is no longer in your best interest. From your perspective, the equation was simple: right equals whatever is good for Brad Howard. Today that means getting a good job and starting a career. Yesterday it meant selling drugs. Even now you can announce without irony, "I feel good to be a black male."

In some sense, I cannot fault you for your views. Like many other young people, you spent twelve years in school, but you got an attitude adjustment instead of an education. You were taught to feel good about yourself and to be proud of who you are, no matter what. On the surface, the idea seems sensible enough: young African Americans do not succeed because they are not taught that they can succeed. For the past thirty years, education experts have noted that young people like you are constantly bombarded by negative images of black men and women on television, in the movies, and in your neighborhoods. They have also pushed the idea that these images are holding you back. So instead of rewarding real success and discouraging failure, they decided to bolster your self-esteem. But rather than building self-esteem, educators have taught a generation of young people to parrot the phrases of "empowerment." Almost without exception, every young African American I have met says he is proud of himself. Even you are proud. And almost without exception, all of those young people cannot answer the simple question, "Why are you proud of yourself?"

Educators have ignored the obvious fact that real self-esteem comes only from real accomplishments. Without real accomplishments the phrases you repeat are just empty words. What is worse, words like *pride, courage,* and *respect* have lost their meaning to young people raised on a diet of self-esteem. Just as obscenities no longer shock, the vocabulary of self-esteem no longer inspires. With every accomplishment, no matter how small, now treated as equally important, young people are losing respect for real achievements.

The popularity of Malcolm X is a good example of what this education has done. In my previous letter, I referred to Malcolm's insights on street hustlers. I hoped that his ideas would carry weight because you, like most other African Americans, say you respect him. But let me suggest that you probably should not respect Malcolm, at least not for the reasons you think. I believe Malcolm X is the most misunderstood black hero in America. As one young looter during the L.A. riots said on "Nightline," "King— King fought for peace, but you don't get nothing by just talking. I believe in Malcolm X's way. I don't believe in turning the cheek. We've been turning the cheek for far too long. Now it's time for retaliation." From political leaders to street hustlers to rap singers, Malcolm is lionized for one phrase: "By any means necessary." It has become the battle cry of every black hoodlum who wants to loot a store and the campaign theme of every black politician who wants to stir up his constituents. Although I disagree with much of what Malcolm believed, I am profoundly saddened that this man's life and all he stood for has been reduced to a slogan on a T-shirt and a way to justify violence.

There is much about Malcolm X's life that deserves respect. Like you, he began as a street hustler and a thief. But instead of making excuses for his behavior, he turned his life around. It is true that he talked of liberating African Americans "by any means necessary," but what were those means? He demanded abstinence from premarital sex and alcohol. He required his followers to study intensely. He did not tolerate drugs—either using or selling them; he called them poison. He condemned the lust for the material things you covet. Malcolm's message is perfectly clear: stop selling drugs, stop living in sin, take responsibility for your children, do not smoke or drink, work hard and study harder. As Malcolm would quickly explain, those are the "means" that are necessary.

Instead, Malcolm's misguided modern followers like to think he justified violence. To my knowledge, nothing Malcolm ever said or did could reasonably be used to justify the sort of street hustler violence that rap singers and high school cowards so admire. As I mentioned in my last letter, Malcolm wrote that your sort of violence "scared" him. I wonder if the young African Americans I see walking around Washington with Malcolm X's image on their backs have ever tried, or even know how, to live the kind of life he demanded. I disagree with many of Malcolm's views. He believed that America is a hopelessly racist country in which black people will never succeed. He believed it is better for black people to separate themselves from the larger culture and viewed the whole idea of integration as white scam. I know from my own experience that he was wrong on both counts. But I do know that he was right in first insisting that anyone who wants to improve society must first look at the man in the mirror. Humans are social creatures, and you are the element of society you are responsible for. How do you treat your neighbors? By selling drugs to them? Using them for sex? Occasionally offing one? You can't condemn the corruption or flaws of a society when you spend your time helping to destroy it. You can do the most to improve society by improving yourself.

The moral demands Malcolm X placed on himself and his followers are more than admirable; they are what is most essential to improve the lot of each black brother and sister in America. But it is also the most difficult thing in the world to change. It is much easier to point out the mite in the eye of the rest of the world than to deal with the plank in our own.

In many ways, he and Martin Luther King, Jr., had more in common that most young people realize. Like Malcolm, Dr. King was a deeply religious man who demanded much from himself and those who followed him. Dr. King and Malcolm X both realized that self-esteem comes from self-respect, and that both have to be earned through hard work and a dedication to living a moral life. How far we have moved away from those principles! Today the "civil rights establishment" is all about what kind of special treatment America owes blacks as a result of its racist past, rather than about what we can do to get beyond that. We push for a legalized racial spoils system called affirmative action, which, in principle, is just another shade of the old Jim Crow laws. We talk about "reparations." From whom? People who never held slaves. For whom? People who never were slaves.

Meanwhile, we set up our own children for bitter disappointment by trying to fill them up with empty self-esteem. We think that if we teach kids to feel good about themselves, perhaps real accomplishments will follow. That approach is exactly backward. Both Malcolm and Dr.

King would have agreed that each of us should understand our own inherent worth as beloved children of God. Beyond that, both would measure a man or woman by how hard he or she struggles to follow God's laws and improve himself or herself. Esteem is a high regard or opinion for someone. Real self-esteem comes from making oneself worthy to be esteemed, but today it is in fashion to teach young people that just showing up is enough. Our children are in for an awful shock if we send them into the world with a baseless high regard for themselves.

I know that many black leaders disagree with me. Many believe that the history of victimization puts children at an emotional disadvantage that needs to be countered with as much positive encouragement as possible. They also believe that planting the seeds of self-esteem at an early age is necessary to counter the negative attitudes and experiences of racism they are likely to encounter. These people do have a point: many young black children have a hard time finding positive role models, and American culture is often willing to ignore the contributions African Americans have made. When I did a program on the D-Day invasion, for example, I had on my radio program my friend and mentor Senator Strom Thurmond, who had fought in World War II. Many people called the station afterward to criticize me for not bringing black war heroes on my show. At one level, I was distressed that so many of my listeners still see everything, even the anniversary of this historic day, in racial terms. On another level, though, I could appreciate their desire to publicize the accomplishments of black Americans. But even as I agree with this desire, I have to note that none of it makes a big of difference when it comes to the philosophy of self-esteem.

Even if our history textbooks and newspapers were filled with the accomplishments of black Americans, it would not build genuine self-esteem among young African Americans. Imagine how silly it would sound if white people went around saying, "I am a personal success because I am white and Leonardo da Vinci was white." Anyone who made such a statement would be dismissed as an idiot by all of the white people I know. Yet this is precisely what black intellectuals have accomplished by teaching self-esteem to black children. Our young people are encouraged to believe that the heroic efforts of Harriet Tubman make them better people. Please. Harriet Tubman's accomplishments made *her* a good person. That is all. If we want young African Americans to feel good about themselves, we should teach them calculus in high school and reward them when they put forward the effort and perform to the best of their abilities. Worst of all, habituating children to maintain an unearned sense of self-satisfaction destroys the best incentive for real accomplishment and discourages the motivation that leads to all real achievement.

I am barely old enough to recall the time when we first heard that black was beautiful. In the early 1960s black America was just beginning to emerge from the legacy of Jim Crow. In the South blacks attended separate schools, drank out of separate drinking fountains, used separate toilets, and ate in separate restaurants. Whites made sure these accommodations were separate because they did not want to be soiled by the black people around them. Everywhere I turned were signs that America believed African Americans were dirty, unworthy, and somehow less than fully human. In the early 1960s, our parents' generation rebelled against these attitudes and asserted our humanity. Back then when black people began saying "Black is beautiful," they meant that black is no less beautiful than white, that we are all equal in the eyes of God. Today that phrase has been perverted to mean that being black is, in itself, enough to make you good and worthy.

I have often wondered why people of our race embraced this philosophy so quickly and completely. It is not as though some charismatic African-American leader persuaded the public that false pride was the true salvation of the black race. From Frederick Douglass to Malcolm X, every true black leader has stressed the principles of self-discipline and hard work. They have rightly objected to white America's refusal to acknowledge our accomplishments and virtues, but they never suggested that being black is a virtue. Perhaps the answer is as simple as your own life suggests: making race a virtue is far easier than trying to instill true virtues in our young people. Whatever the reason, the effort that began as a way to eliminate prejudice against African Americans has become the anchor of false pride.

This educational fad for self-esteem training, like so many other social and educational experiments performed on young American school children, has backfired. Well-intentioned people have used American children, and especially African Americans like you, as a proving ground for new ideas. I am sickened when I think about the criminal justice reform that dumped hundreds of thousands of violent criminals back into black neighborhoods in the name of rehabilitation, or the mental health reforms that dumped legions of former mental patients into those same neighborhoods, or poorly conceived and executed welfare programs that have encouraged the breakdown of poor families. Young African Americans are always the first to get free condoms in schools, free needles for drug addicts, and subsidized abortions for teens. It is as if society says to itself, "Why not try it in the inner city? After all, things can't get much worse there." But the experience of the past several decades indicates clearly that life can get worse even in the worst neighborhoods. You would be hard pressed to find anyone in America—white or black—who would not trade the illegitimacy rates of today for the rates in 1960, or the crime rates today for the crime rates in 1960, back when laws and attitudes were much more racist than they are today.

Political leaders, both black and white, have not been content merely to eliminate the obstacles to black success. They have sought to engineer our future—and just below all of that engineering lies the assumption that black people cannot handle this future without the help of government. It is this condescending "compassion" and enervating assistance, much more than overt hostility, that has sucked the marrow of black communities in America.

Through the curriculum of self-esteem we have made a policy of pretending that any accomplishment, no matter how trivial, is worthy of praise. In doing so we have undermined the value of real success. That same curriculum pretends that failure does not exist except in the most extreme cases. Your life serves as a clear, if unfortunate, example of this trend. Just by showing up to school each morning more or less regularly for twelve years, you received a high school diploma. I do not mean to offend you when I say that you should have learned a great deal more in twelve years of school than you did, and if you refused to learn you should have failed. Instead the educators who were paid to teach you academic subjects taught you that almost any fault can be overlooked and almost any effort is sufficient. No wonder you find it difficult to summon the discipline required to stay off the streets; you were never even required to finish your homework.

Sometimes this idea of hollow success produces some tragically ludicrous scenes. Each year, the mayor of Washington and other national luminaries hold a luncheon to "honor" a handful of girls who have "learned to practice self-respect and self-control" by agreeing not to have sex while they are enrolled in a program to promote abstinence. This past year the luncheon was attended by some of the nation's most influential women, including the vice president's wife, the wife of Virginia's governor, and the reigning Miss America. These 173 teen and preteen girls are being honored for the profound accomplishment of remaining virgins while they are in the program. I think many people must have been amused, as I was, by the entire spectacle. There stood the mayor of our nation's capital and many of the most important women in the nation appreciatively unveiling the last 173 teenaged virgins in the Washington area.

Talk about meaningless self-esteem! Now, teaching sexual restraint to kids is both admirable and necessary. But most professors of, say, physics are never honored with a luncheon organized by such luminaries. For young African-American girls, however, just keeping their pants on through high school earns them this honor. Honoring these girls undermines years of struggle against prejudice by admitting, in effect, that most young African Americans are no more able to control their sexual urges than most animals. The racist impulse in white America is reinforced by these displays. Once again, well-intentioned public figures had announced to the world that African Americans should not be held to the same standards of self-discipline and self-control we expect from others in our society. For blacks, they seem to say, retaining one's virginity through most (though not all) of their teenage years is nothing short of heroic, and it deserves the personal attention of Miss America, the wife of the vice president, and the highest elected official of our nation's capital.

If the curriculum of self-esteem robs young people of the drive to succeed, its twin, the philosophy of blame, provides them with an excuse for almost any failure. Together they comprise a philosophic outlook that says, "All my actions are worthy; all my deficiencies are the fault of others." Our culture of victimization has become so accepted that when it is occasionally put on public display, few people realize just how absurd it all sounds. I recall African-American leaders, such as Representative Maxine Waters, who defended rioters during the Los Angeles riots on the basis of "joblessness and despair." They agreed that the entire riot was unfortunate but a natural reaction to racism. During the NAACP's ill-conceived gang summit in 1992, Ben Chavis invited street hustlers and murderers to justify selling drugs as a natural reaction to their lack of "hope." Even child abuse in poor black families is excused as the result of the "frustration" poor African-American parents feel. If you are poor and black in America, there is no crime you can commit, no boundary you can cross, that cannot be excused on account of poverty, racism, or general psychological stress.

It does not take much for this philosophy to give way to the kind of selfishness I see in young hustlers such as yourself. After all, if nothing is your fault, then you have no faults. If anything you do can be explained and justified by forces beyond your control, then there is no reason to control your impulses. After a time, the idea that anything one does can be justified gives way to the notion that nothing you do even needs to be justified—at least not to anyone but yourself. It does not take long for the values your parents taught to vanish. This false pride is combined with the constant focus on the "self" in self-esteem to help create the sort of self-centered attitude I see in you. I have to wonder if your days as a street hustler are what those same political leaders have in mind when they proclaim that the eighties were a decade of selfishness and greed. Probably not.

As I look back on my own life, I realize that I was fortunate to have been raised as I was. I grew up on a farm in Marion, South Carolina. It seemed all we did was work. We were up at the break of dawn, feeding the cattle, slopping the pigs, or tending to the fields. I recall one summer day when I had to bring in the tobacco from the fields. It had rained the night before, and by midday the heat and the humidity seemed unbearable. My father had given me several rows of tobacco to finish. When I whined and told him that it was too much, he bent down and explained to me, "Those are your rows. They are yours to do. If you don't make it through those rows, you won't make it through life."

Those rows of tobacco seemed endless. But I knew my father, and I knew that he would not listen to any further complaints, so I got back to work. At that moment I hated the work, and I was angry with my father for making me do it. Between plants I would stop to rest for a few seconds, but that only prolonged my time in the sun. The dust clouded my eyes and got in my clothes. My hair was matted by the dirt and the sweat, and my head pounded in the heat. If it had been an option, I probably would have quit, but I did not have a choice. After what seemed like an eternity, I finally reached the end of the last row. I looked over to my father. He did not say anything; he just smiled and walked with me to the tobacco barn. I knew he was proud of me—not because I was able to work in the tobacco fields but because I did not quit.

That afternoon I learned that real self-respect grows out of little victories. My father was like that. He placed the greatest importance in the smallest things. From getting good grades in math to finishing my chores, he viewed almost everything in the context of a larger picture. Every life is made up of those small decisions, those little victories and defeats, that we deal with every day. Every little, unheralded choice is a piece of the bigger picture—the general direction your life will take. If we are not faithful in the little things, then we cannot be faithful in the larger things. That is why he did not cut slack for my little slips and failings. He felt a great responsibility as our father. As important, he had a keen insight into character—both how it is formed and the role it plays in our lives. It is this insight that he has passed along to me, and which I am now trying to pass on to you.

Getting up, going to work, giving everything your best effort: these are the foundation of real character and, consequently, real self-esteem. My work in the fields does not seem like much now, but the self-respect I gained by completing those rows of tobacco was genuine. Although I would never have finished my chore if my father had not demanded it, the accomplishment was still mine. Looking back on it, I think I felt better about finishing those rows of tobacco than I did graduating from college. In many respects, I think finishing those rows was far more important to the success I enjoy today.

I wonder how differently I might have approached my life if my father had said on that hot summer day, "Don't worry about it, Armstrong. It is good enough that you came out here to the fields to try. You should be proud of that." Even as I write those words, I realize how ridiculous they are. My father knew better. Yet every day teachers, parents, and politicians say those very words to people like you. When your father bought you a car and continued your monthly allowance even though you were hustling, he was telling you that just showing up was good enough. When your parents put up their house as collateral so they could bail you out of jail and then stood silent as you continued to deal drugs, they were telling you that just showing up was good enough. When your school gave you a high school diploma even though you can barely speak basic English they were telling you that just showing up was good enough. And when your girl-friend and newborn daughter stayed with you even though you were running around with other women, she too was telling you that just showing up was good enough. These people who never demand anything from you say they are trying to help, but all the while they are robbing you of an opportunity to earn even the most modest real self-respect.

While the philosophy of self-esteem prevents many young people from gaining self-respect, it also robs others of the respect they have earned. You said to me, "I had a lot of respect on the street." I would have laughed at that comment except that I have heard so many young people say they "respect" street hustlers. As Malcolm X observed of his time on the streets, the highest respect goes to the most reckless and vicious hoodlum—the "craziest nigger." The virtues normal society encourages in its members are twisted to fit the hustling lifestyle and then held up to younger or less reckless hustlers as a model. Courage becomes recklessness. Independence is reduced to con-tempt. Ambition and drive are transformed into selfish-ness and greed. Bravery becomes self-destruction. The words, and the world, are turned upside down, and many young people do not even know it.

In this world, there is no room to recognize real courage, drive, ambition, or independence. So while other young people you knew were busy admiring your fancy cars and your ghetto courage, they were ignoring or ridi-culing people who worked in so-called dead-end jobs. Without a moral compass to help them distinguish between real and empty accomplishments, they looked only at the material results of each. Because so few young people are taught the real meaning of dignity, they think the peculiar power wielded by the street hustler has earned him respect. Young people see hustlers like you acting as petty lords: issuing commands, demanding homage from your lieutenants, even setting and enforcing your own legal code. As you bragged to me, you were able to have someone killed if you wished; you "had a lot of power." Thanks to millions of men who have abandoned their children, many young African Americans who grow up in the city will be exposed to your kind of power and respect, and it is the only example they will ever see.

You should have known better. Even while he was making it easy for you to do the wrong thing, your own father was living a life that deserves real respect. To this day, you say you respect your father. Why? What about him do you respect? Your father is just another working-class black man stuck in a job that is going nowhere. He has spent all of his life working, and what has he gotten for it? Unlike you, your father would never get the respect of your former friends on the street. Unlike you, your father would never have women lining up to win his affections. Unlike you, your father would never be able to tell someone in his "crew" to "take care of" one of his enemies. By the measure of the street thug, you, Brad, had a lot of power; your father has none. If he were not your own father, I think you might call him a chump.

Still, you are beginning to understand that his wasn't a dead-end job but an opportunity to provide an honest living. Even with all of your money and your "power," you could never earn his respect, and you could never recreate the dignity that he has. That, Brad, is why you and your brother were dead to him. You had lost his respect.

I think your young admirers would be surprised if they knew the truth about you and your father. He can see right through your false pride, your empty success, and your recklessness. Teenagers in the ghetto think that hustlers who carry guns and face death are courageous. Only you knew how scared you really were. You told me about it, but you could never tell your boys back home about it. For them, you have to put up a front, put on a show, because your life depends on the face you show. Living as a predator, living with predators, any sign of weakness is fatal. So you and all your friends live on the edge of the abyss day in and day out, never looking down, pretending not to notice. Inside, this life eats you up, which is why you said you wanted out. Yet looking back on your life, even you admit that you took the easy way out. As dangerous as dealing drugs could be, it was much easier to live for yourself, for the moment and for money, than to take responsibility for your actions and live as your father did: working hard, providing for your children, reining in your impulses. Even today, it is difficult for you to face the struggle and real sacrifices that such a life requires. Unlike carrying a gun and walking the streets, living a respectable life demands genuine courage.

I warned you in my last letter that you will not get much encouragement as you try to change your life. One clear reason is that by rejecting the false pride that has anchored you in the past, you are announcing to your former friends that they are not leading good lives. By changing, you are implicitly holding them accountable for still leading that life and condemning the damage they do. To make matters tougher, you must turn away from the streets in shame rather than victory. You should feel bad about the way you have lived. You should be ashamed of how you have wasted the opportunities people have given you. You should be ashamed and embarrassed by the way you used women. You should lose your false self-respect, and along with it you should lose forever the hollow respect you had for your street hustler friends. None of this is easy to do. It is a very hard thing to renounce your past, because you have to assume the heavy responsibility of your actions. But renounce it you must, if you are to have any future at all.

In so doing, you will have achieved one of those small victories I talked about earlier. Your decision itself is a real accomplishment. You have given up the streets so you can provide for your children. In exchange, your daughters will see in you a bit of the dignity you admire in your own father. That is no small reward. And if you manage to break from the streets completely, one day you will feel good to be Brad Howard rather than feeling good to be "a black male."

Sincerely,

Armstrong

Chapter Four

"The Other Race"

Dear Brad:

In my last letter I told you that I believe educators and the urban culture are discouraging young African Americans from gaining real self-respect. Those problems certainly are not unique to young blacks, but yours are compounded by the added social pressures against independent thought and individuality in the black community. As a young black man you must be ready when your African-American sisters and brothers play the race card.

When you turn your back on the streets, some people will accuse you of "not acting black,"—even as you have said the same about people. They will say about you what you said about your friend the policewoman: "She act like the other race. She act like she white now." Others will try to discourage you by saying that there is no way for a black man to get ahead in America and that the only ones who do are "Toms." They will play on racial stereotypes and exploit your racial fears. It is not that they hope you will fail. Rather, your success will undermine their own best excuse for failure: the ghost of racism.

Now please do not misunderstand me. I know there is racism in America. I grew up in South Carolina where I saw aggressive, ugly racism translated into deeds. But having seen the real thing, I am not so quick to find racism in every perceived slight, and I have little tolerance for people who use it as an excuse for their own failures. It is often easier to blame racism for the problems you encounter than it is to look honestly at yourself. Even among some successful African-American professionals I know, there is an automatic tendency to blame racism whenever something goes wrong. It is because the boss is racist, they say, that they failed to get promoted. Racist clients prevent them from making a sale or gaining a lucrative contract. It is a tempting trap.

In our conversations I also heard you making some of the same comments. You attributed to racism the "smart little comments" you heard your coworkers at the trade association "saying under their breath." As you told me, you were working at the trade association and at the same time hustling at night. You said you often had trouble getting to work because you had been out selling drugs until the early hours of the morning. Did it ever occur to you that those comments might have been prompted by the fact that you were coming in late, that you were obviously tired, and that you probably were not doing a very good job? I was not there, of course, but I would bet pennies to dollars that the comments you heard had nothing to do with your race. But assume they did. So what? You will encounter racist people as you try to move away from the streets. There is very little you can do about that. Like all other African Americans, you are faced with an unfair choice: work around the prejudice you find or let it be a barrier that keeps you down. In your day-to-day life, that is the choice you have to make.

Let me tell you about how my own parents viewed race, and how this shaped my opinions. My brothers and sisters, like me, never get caught up in race because my dad always taught us that you've got to judge a person by his or her heart. He felt that if we armed ourselves with knowledge and humility, there was nothing that we could not do. My mother, like so many other black women raised in the South back then, was the pessimist. She always thought that white people were only going to let you go so far. She distrusted white people right off, and she wasn't going to give any of them a chance any more than she thought they would give her one.

One day my mom was staying with me at my home, and I told her I was expecting a guest. When he arrived, she answered the door and told the fellow standing there that he must be at the wrong address—because the last thing she expected was that he would be white. If he stayed, she said, she was going to leave. She didn't feel comfortable in the house with a white man. Well, I thought about it for a minute, then told my mom that my friend had flown in from New York and that she was just going to have to leave because I was not going accommodate her racism. She wasn't happy at first, but at the end of the weekend she told me she was happy that it worked out. She admitted that I had helped her become a better person.

Right now racism (either your own or someone else's)

is the least of your problems. Your most difficult task will be to convince people, both black and white, that you have really changed. When you get suspicious looks, when you have a hard time finding people who are willing to hire you, when you hear your coworkers talking under their breath, it will not be because you are a black man but because you still talk and act a lot like a street hustler. Whenever you are tempted to use racism to explain a problem, think first of how you must appear to others. You may not know it, but the murderer you once were still reveals himself in your conversations, your stories, and your attitude. I have noticed it, and I think others will as well.

When I asked you whether you held any hatred or resentment toward white people in general, you told me no, not anymore. But then you added casually, "Like two years ago, I'd have killed them." Tell me, do you really believe that the white people you worked with, even the few you knew socially, didn't understand that you perceived them as different because of their race? Do you think that hostility toward them would go unnoticed? Don't you think that affected the way they treated you?

Let's not forget, Brad, that you were a dangerous man. More important, you came to embody everything that American society has grown to fear about young black men. People had a reason to fear you. I don't call that racism. For very sensible reasons, you fear those thugs who kidnapped you. It's just as sensible for anyone, white or black, to suspect, or even fear the Brad Howards of the world.

You and I both know how hard it is for a black man to hail a taxi here in D.C.—not because the drivers are racist (most of them are black) but because hundreds of cab drivers have been robbed or murdered by black men. We shouldn't condemn the cab drivers; we should condemn those among our people who behave like beasts.

Deep down, I think you understand this; it's to your credit that you bear no hated toward white people, just as it is to your credit that you no longer want to be viewed as a "crazy nigger." You won't be able to escape the suspicion completely; stereotypes (right or wrong) about black men are too ingrained in American culture right now. You can, however, be sure that you do everything possible to ensure that the people who get to know Brad Howard the individual respect you because they see that you respect yourself.

What concerns me far more than any prejudice you will find among whites is the prejudice you have against our own people. You seem to share a common view of many urban African Americans that being black means acting like a hustler and talking like a slave. "I know how to talk white," you told me. "You know, all proper like." Where did you get the idea that speaking decent English had anything to do with being white? After Frederick Douglass escaped from slavery, he became one of America's most accomplished speakers and political writers. His English prose was much more "proper" than that of most white people I know. W. E. B. du Bois graduated from Harvard in 1896 speaking far better English than most white Americans. From Booker T. Washington to Dr. King, black leaders have spoken and written some of the most compelling words in America. Not one of them was "talking white."

It is not that I care so much how well you speak (though using proper English will help you in your career) but that

I find in your attitude a slave mentality that should have vanished long ago. The idea that blacks speak in broken, semiliterate English is an idea that was invented and spread by white slaveholders who were trying to prove that blacks were inferior. The same is true of your attitude about the way black people ought to act. Who passed the law requiring black people to be promiscuous, talk loud, take drugs, and brawl? That is not acting black; that is acting just as nineteenth-century slaveholders would have wanted you to act. Frederick Douglas explained back in 1845,

> It was necessary to keep our [slave] masters unacquainted with the fact that instead of spending the sabbath in wrestling, boxing, and drinking whiskey, we were trying to learn to read the will of God; for they had much rather see us engaged in those degrading sports than to see us behaving like intellectual, moral, and accountable beings.

When you define what it means to "be black" behaviorally, you are, plain and simple, carrying out the will of the people who enslaved your ancestors. I am just not willing to let 130 years of struggle be unraveled by street hustlers who take pride in degradation. You do not need to start talking or acting "white" to succeed, but you do need to stop thinking of your own race in the way a slaveholder would.

I do not wish to be too hard on you here. Your ideas are mostly a reflection of your education and environment—and by education, I mean what you have learned from your peers, role models, and the adults you associated with while growing up. If you are tuned in to the news, white and black intellectuals are constantly trying to justify bad behavior as an expression of blackness. African Americans of all stations are all too willing to dismiss those of us who make it out of poverty as sell-outs. All of the self-esteem education to which we subject our young people does nothing to stem the tidal wave of destructive ideas that we foist on ourselves in the name of "authentic blackness."

Think of the way you call yourself a "black male." Why don't you think of yourself as a black man? The term *black male* is something you should use to describe dark-haired animals, not yourself. You are an intellectual, moral, accountable being who deserves the name *man* and all the obligations that go with it. When you think of yourself as a black male, you are reinforcing the idea that you are merely a reasoning animal. Expect more of yourself than that word implies. If I could have one wish for the black community, it would be that no one ever again would use the phrase *acting black* to describe the street hustlers' behavior or use the words *male* and *female* to mean black men and women. Your children need a man to be their father, your girlfriend needs a man to be her husband, and if they want a "black male," they can go out and buy a cat.

A caller to my radio program the other day reminded me of some other folks who will criticize you during your rehabilitation: the conspiracy theorists. I first encountered the idea of a "white conspiracy" shortly after I began my radio show in Washington. At first I thought the caller was merely some flake, so I cut him off and took the next call. During the next several weeks I had dozens of similar calls, and I began talking to other black people in Washington about the subject. I was surprised by how many black people truly believe there is some sort of carefully orchestrated conspiracy against them.

Here in D.C., there have been long-standing rumors about "the Plan"—that is, a secret white conspiracy to keep black people out of power. Considering that virtually all political power, and much of the economic muscle in this city, is in the hands of African Americans, I would say that the Plan, if it exists, is a failure. But the rumors persist. One typical caller to my show challenged me: "You don't really think Mayor Sharon Pratt Kelly has any real power, do you? The real power is behind the scenes." His tone implied, "If you weren't such a fool, you would see that."

Did you hear the one about the clothing brand called Troop? According to the book *Heard It Through the Grapevine,* the company went out of business after someone started a rumor that the name stood for "To Rule Over Oppressed People" and that linings of their clothing contained messages like, "Thank you, nigger, for making us rich." And of course the Nation of Islam, through its "newspaper" the *Final Call,* spreads stories about government plots to sterilize black men or to kill off the black population with AIDS or drugs.

Now you can believe that if you like, Brad. There is no way to disprove any of these rumors, and any attempt to do so is just taken as more evidence for the conspiracy. I would make the case that if there is any conspiracy against our people, it comes from within. It comes from streetcorner drug dealers willing to peddle their poison to any paying customer. It comes from rappers who glorify and justify rape and violence against black women. And it comes, finally, from prominent, visible African Americans who play the race card to excuse all manner of personal failures. You must remember when our mayor, Marion Barry, embarrassed himself, this city, and all black Americans by getting caught on camera smoking crack and sexually propositioning a woman in a posh hotel room. Do you remember his excuses? It was either the fault of the white establishment, or of Barry's woman companion, or both. The most disgraceful moment of the whole affair was the drunk, stoned Barry being led away in handcuffs, slurring over and over, "The goddamn bitch set me up!"

Sadly, this was the refrain of the thousands of African Americans who rushed to defend this man. His incoherent complaints were emblazoned on T-shirts for his supporters to wear. Eventually a mostly black jury decided that the excuses put forth by the mayor and his lawyers were good enough. Blame for Marion Barry's immorality rested on white society and on the women he lusted after, not on his own shoulders. We are not responsible for our actions. It's white America's fault.

You and I both know how feeble this claim is. There was no white man in the room showing Barry how to handle that crack pipe with expertise; that woman used no enchanted potion to win his affection. Marion Barry did what Marion Barry wanted to do—just as you made the choice to begin dealing drugs and just as you made the choice to stop.

These claims of conspiracy do have power. Looking back on the history of our people, someone seeking evidence of a conspiracy would have ample evidence. Between slavery, Jim Crow, and race riots and lynchings,

American society worked against the interests of black people for a long, long time.

You and I are lucky enough to have been born after the worst was over; now, as I can personally attest, there are great opportunities for African Americans in business, government, and every other walk of life. More black families earn middle-class incomes than ever before; black business ownership is on the rise; and in 1994 more blacks than ever ran for (and won) seats in the U.S. Congress.

In spite of these growing opportunities, an increasing number of black men are choosing the criminal road you once walked. Tens of thousands of young black girls are choosing to become mothers before they're barely out of pigtails themselves. At the very time the vast majority of white people are willing to accept us as full partners in American society, we are more and more likely to opt out. What would our forefathers have said? In 1829, black essayist David Walker wrote, "Let no man of us budge one step, and let slaveholders come to beat us from our country. America is more our country, than it is the whites—we have enriched it with our blood and tears. The greatest riches in all America have arisen from our blood and tears."

Walker and thousands, millions, of black Americans fought and struggled against a white majority unwilling to concede them even the most fundamental human rights. Yet they persevered and endured, and ultimately they won. They secured the right for you and me to make our own choices, to make the most of the same opportunities this country has afforded whites for two centuries. It is an insult and a disgrace to what they fought for that today so many young blacks have chosen lives of criminality and degeneracy. What a waste of freedom.

Brad, if you keep focused on your humanity and your goals for your children, I am confident that you will have the strength of character to take responsibility for your own life and to prevail against the many racial pressures you will feel from both African Americans and whites. Remember that racists thrive on breeding fear. And to borrow from a famous "white American," the only thing you have to fear is yourself.

Sincerely,

Armstrong

Chapter Five

"The Mother of My Daughters"

Dear Brad:

When you first bragged to me about the "fifteen hundred women" you have had sex with, I dismissed it as just another example of a street hustler bravado. When I heard the pride in your voice as you described how you had been able to buy their affections with the money you made from drugs, I became disgusted. But when you told me that all this time you had a steady girlfriend who knew about your liaisons and did not care, I was shocked. You seem to view women in much the same way you view Big Macs: when you are hungry you have one, and then you toss the wrapper on the street without giving it another thought. As you bluntly explained about these women, "I don't respect them much." They are useful to have around when you need to satisfy your appetite, but otherwise they are irrelevant, expensive luxuries. It seems that the modern ghetto is the only place in America where the vision of sixties free love pushed by upper-class sex gurus has survived. The "if it feels good, do it" mentality is alive and well but with a ghetto twist: "If it feels good do it, and feel good about doing it."

Over the past several months, I had all but forgotten about this part of your life. I guess I was so consumed by your stories of drug sales and murder that your promiscuous sexual habits seemed to pale by comparison. Then last evening a caller to my radio program said something that reminded me of your comments. The caller was a middle-aged man who was devastated by the fact that his teenage daughter had become pregnant. He had called because he was angry that I had opposed distributing condoms in school, but during the course of our conversation, it became clear that he was not really angry with me as much as he was furious with you and other young men like you.

He was the father of three children, two girls and a boy. His oldest daughter had recently turned sixteen, and now she was pregnant. I asked him if he knew the young father, and he responded with a quiet "no." Then he quickly added, "All of the kids are having sex these days. You just can't avoid it. You are crazy to think that by you telling them no they'll quit." I had great sympathy for this man. He has spent sixteen years trying his best to be a good father. He told me that he and his family lived in a comfortable northern Virginia suburb. As he spoke, I could envision a working-class man a lot like your own father— someone doing his best to help his children build a better life. The fact that he was there, living with his family and trying to support them, proved he was already a far better man than most of those you know.

I could not blame him for being angry. In just a few minutes one evening, some teenager robbed his daughter of the opportunities this man had spent a lifetime trying to provide. Now she is about to become a single teenage mother, and the odds are stacked against her. She may never finish high school; it will now be extremely difficult for her to go to college and nearly impossible for her to have a meaningful career. She is the one who will pay most dearly for unmarried sex. She faces years of hardship as she tries to raise a child alone. If she is lucky, she will get the bare material support you provide your own children: some money from time to time and some affection when you are in the mood to give it. More likely she will have no support from this young man. In the future she will find it much harder to get married or even fall in love; it is not easy to find time for romance when you have an infant at home.

Some of the callers to my radio program suggested that the "solution" to this girl's problem is abortion, sex education, or, as this man tried to argue, free condoms. I wonder if he truly thought that the reason his daughter became pregnant had anything to do with the fact that she could not find a condom. I suppose if I had pressed him on the point, he would have admitted that even if his "little girl" had a box of condoms in her purse, it would not have made any difference. Just listening to you, I think it is a pretty safe bet that the young man who fathered this child did not wear a condom because he did not want to wear one. Had he wanted to protect this girl from pregnancy, or AIDS, he could have walked into any drugstore in the neighborhood.

Now the fact that this young man did not care whether his girlfriend was protected probably shows nothing more than that he was a typical teenager, careless and generally irresponsible. That is nothing unique to him, or to black teenagers in general. This same attitude is equally prevalent in white middle-class and upper-class communities around the country. The assumption, the expectation, is that young girls and young men will have sex and that the young man has little or no responsibility for the consequences. More than that, there is in some quarters an attitude that having an illegitimate baby is a cause for pride rather than a mark of irresponsibility. For young women like this caller's daughter, even the example her parents set is not enough to override the relentless message from outside the family that becoming a single mother is gratifying and noble.

As the father of three girls, I would expect you to worry about this kind of attitude. Most men I know are very protective of their daughters, and to a person they all admit that the reason is that they remember how they acted and thought when they were young. You do not seem to show any of that same protectiveness. Neither does your girlfriend. In fact, as shocked as I am about how your view of women, I am even more surprised that your girlfriend has tolerated your years of acting like an alley cat while she raises your children. Even now, she has not demanded that you be faithful to her. Instead, she is satisfied with an arrangement where you "see each other most every day."

I will admit that I have decidedly unenlightened views of sex. My religion regards sex as a sacramental act expressing a total and lifelong commitment between two individuals—that commitment being necessary for the natural result of the act, children. Because our sexuality is so integral a component of each of us, its indiscriminate use or misuse damages us. Yet because it is such a passionate and primal drive, it is easily abused. That is why sexual behavior has always been subject to strong social taboos. The abuse of sex can wound the participants, and almost certainly it will severely impair the generation that results from it. The sexual union is the source of permanency in any society, because it is the source of its renewal.

But I do not think your attitude is what anyone had in mind when they preached the virtues of sexual liberation. Today I find that most young men and women, especially those living in the ghetto, are willing accomplices in the most empty, irresponsible kind of relationships. You judge women (and your women friends judge men) in the same way a banker evaluates a loan: if they are a good risk and you can get something out of them, you do business. It's nothing personal.

During our interviews you explained this attitude as clearly as anyone could. In one sentence, you talked with great admiration about the older, churchgoing women you know, and in the next you admitted that you respected them because they "stood behind" you when you were on trial. You appreciate your girlfriend because she is "the mother of my daughters," and you appreciate the women who slept with you.

To an outside observer, the most striking element about these transactions between young men and women in the ghetto is the contempt they engender between the parties. Whether you are mocking your mother's values even as you say you "respect" her, or sleeping around on your girlfriend even as you say you "love" her, it is clear that you could care less about either of them. It is also clear that the feeling is mutual—at least between you and your girlfriend. After all, you can visit her and your daughters only when she allows it, and she has told you explicitly that she feels no obligation toward you if you get in trouble with other hustlers or the law. The same contempt was clear in the women you used to sleep with. You would buy them presents and they would sleep with you, but, as you said, they were more than willing to set you up for another drug dealer or the police if they got a better deal.

In your world, women trade sex for the things they desire, and men trade money, drugs, or prestige for sex. Both sides publicly market their assets until they find a "buyer" and the exchange is made. When the middle class stares in disbelief as people like you spend what little money you have to buy flashy clothes and expensive cars, it is because they do not understand the market for sex. This philosophy has become so entrenched that I often hear young people being asked to justify their relationships in terms of what they "got" out of the deal. It is common for a young ghetto woman to ask another why she is "with" some particular young man. If she replies that he treats her right, by which she often means he buys her things and takes her to nice places, her friend will inevitably admit that she is justified. The answer is unassailable. Even a more trivial answer like "he's all right" is acceptable as long as it is followed by a promise that she is actively looking for something better to come along.

And this attitude is hardly limited to younger people. As I was standing in line at a grocery store near your neighborhood the other night, I heard a woman in her early forties express a similar sentiment. She and a friend were glancing through the bridal magazines at the checkout stand. The two women compared notes on what they liked in wedding clothes, and then this woman remarked, "I'm ready to get married. I have my dress picked out and the church picked out. I have decided on everything. All I have to do is find a man." The two friends laughed at this comment, and then the woman continued, "I have been married four times, and this time I want it to be right." But she was not talking about the marriage; she was talking about the *wedding*! It was the fun of getting married that she sought, and in exchange she was willing to offer her fifth husband regular sex for as long as they both shall enjoy it.

This transaction-based dating is all very nice and neat. In some sense it even empowers women, who can at least be very open about what they expect to get in exchange for their attentions. One could even argue that such an arrangement is the ultimate expression of sexual liberation: people are able to have sex when, where, and with whom they choose and both parties agree beforehand about the conditions of the exchange. But, Brad, this arrangement exacts an extremely high price from young people like you. With each transaction, you surrender a bit of your humanity, and with each transaction you diminish the humanity of the women you know. Even now, you refer to your girlfriend as something less than an actual human being. Are you aware that throughout our conservations you have never once mentioned her name? She is just "the mother of my daughters" or "my girlfriend." It is as if the only way you can describe her is in terms of her usefulness to you— a mother or a lover—rather than as a person.

More than any other thing you have said to me, your attitude about women and relationships leaves me discouraged about your future. I suppose I should not be bothered by it. After all, in the street hustler's world, this view is completely consistent and largely predictable. Hustlers view almost all other people as objects that can be traded, co-opted, avoided, or eliminated. But my thoughts are haunted by the idea that applying these standards to the women in your life is fundamentally different. It is as if you have broken through the barrier protecting the one last fortress of your humanity. If you cannot love even your lovers, I do not know how you will ever begin to find value in your life beyond the streets, and I do not know how you and your girlfriend will ever be able to create a family.

To be fair, the women who share your bed must also share some of the responsibility for the destruction of inner-city families. I know that it is fashionable to blame the entire problem on "deadbeat dads" and to focus on young black men as the chief source of urban violence, but many young women have become enablers who tolerate and even encourage your behavior. It is substantially true that the greatest reward that comes to a successful street hustler is his appeal to young ghetto women. More than the nice cars or the other material things he accumulates and far more than the ego-boosting power he feels as he commands his "crew," the street hustler's behavior is encouraged by the women who admire his daring and even his brutality. I do not want to blame women for your behavior, but I do think that there is no faster way to discourage young men from being self-destructive than for these women to demand better.

This observation is hardly new. In most cultures, women are a civilizing force that serves to restrain the destructive habits of young men. In the modern ghetto, however, the traditional role is not only abandoned but actively opposed. I have heard one young woman ask another why she was "messin'" with her husband, by which she meant why hadn't she dumped him, after this young wife explained that she and her husband had not been getting along and that she was unhappy. I was amazed that this woman had to defend the fact that she did not immediately cast off this man to whom she had made a commitment just because their relationship was going badly. The ghetto attitude encourages young women to write off men at the first sign of trouble, and any woman who is reluctant to do that is perceived by other women as weak and dependent. Coupled with the belief that fathers are all but irrelevant to the raising of children and that even good fathers provide nothing more than financial support, most of the impulse women have to stay with a particular man is destroyed. Just as the ghetto hustler takes false pride in his violent behavior, ghetto women take false pride in their obstinate independence. The idea that any sign of commitment or dependence on a man is a sign of weakness practically eliminates any possibility of the kind of relationship your parents have.

It is understandable that these women would feel especially vulnerable if they became dependent on a man like you. But with women refusing to express any lasting loyalty to a particular man and men using that as an excuse to avoid making any sort of lasting commitment, both groups have shut out the other. With both men and women now believing that they are self-sufficient, self-contained units, each begins to look toward the other for only the most temporary kind of gratification. As a result, these women, intentionally or not, encourage young men to be destructive because they create an environment where the wildest among the young men are also the most sexually appealing. And why not? If the woman believes she is entering into only a short-term, mutually gratifying transaction, she allows herself to find satisfaction in hooking up with whoever seems most amusing at the time.

In some sense, the hustler's appeal lies in his image as a modern-day pirate—a buccaneer who is man enough to take what he wants. That kind of imagery appeals to women and men far outside the confines of the inner city. The romance novels voraciously consumed by so many women often feature this type of character, and the heroine inevitably falls under his spell. But for most people, it remains just a fantastic image, and the desire for pirates becomes less important than the desire for a respectable man. When middle-class fantasies give way to the real world, pirates are seen not as romantic figures but as murderers and thugs. When confronted by a choice between the sort of real-life pirate you represented when you were on the streets and the type of man your father is, black women of your mother's generation could always be counted on to choose your father. But no more. Now the preference seems to have shifted as young black women no longer respect the virtues of honesty, loyalty, and hard work above the excitement and danger of the criminal.

These women don't respect themselves as women. Just as they feel inferior, they want someone from the sewer to share their bed. Under all the bravado and tough talk, too many black women don't think they deserve anything better than a common street hood.

If the pirate image or the promise of some kind of material payment provides the initial attraction, most ongoing relationships are merely low-cost, mutually acceptable transactions. As I have listened to you talk, I have wondered if you and your friends are even capable of love— free or otherwise. You say you love your girlfriend, but what does that mean? You have never made any sort of commitment to one another, and neither of you seems willing to sacrifice, even in the smallest degree, for the sake of the other. As near as I can tell from what you have said to me, you and your girlfriend are little more than friends who sleep together from time to time. You do not depend on one another for support, and both of you seem to prefer the arrangement that way. There is little, if any, trust between you, and your connection to one another is so weak that it cannot withstand even the most modest demands. The mother of your children does not even feel confident enough (or she does not care enough) in your relationship to demand that you stop dealing drugs.

The implications of this kind of relationship go well beyond your life with your girlfriend. There may be near-unanimous agreement that many of the problems we see in the inner city can be traced to the disintegration of families, but the families themselves cannot be repaired if the idea of love has been reduced to mutually agreeable transactions between young men and women.

Beyond the women who serve your sexual needs stands another group of women who seem all too willing to encourage your behavior: the older women in your neighborhood. I find it remarkable that your mother's friends, knowing that you have been, in your own words, "terrorizing" their children and grandchildren, knowing that you were selling drugs to their neighbors and preying on their daughters, consistently came to your defense when you were finally caught by the police. This phenomenon was clearly presented in this year's election in Washington, D.C., when Mayor Barry made shorter prison sentences and faster parole one of his key campaign promises. Women your mother's age voted for him in force even though the prisoners Mayor Barry intends to parole will quickly return to their practice of selling drugs to their children.

Thus contradictory behavior is incomprehensible to middle-class Americans, both black and white, but it is completely predictable. As I explained in an earlier letter, the constant focus on racism, both real and imagined, has left people your mother's age more fearful of the judicial system than of the murderers in their midst. Thanks in large part to the media and black political leaders, we have arrived at a point where it would seem just short of traitorous for black women and men to demand longer, swifter, or harsher penalties for black criminals. The relentless message that it is not their fault and that the real problem is a lack of adequate social programs has seemed to transform protecting young hustlers into a virtue. Combined with the popular view that this ghetto behavior is the "authentic" black voice, these attitudes have become a powerful destructive force.

These older women have always been the source of

strength in the black community. But they too have become accustomed to the idea that your approach to sex and relationships is normal. It is not. To upper-class white and black Americans, the sexual revolution has meant a more eventful ride through puberty and a skyrocketing abortion rate. It is generally regarded as something to be discouraged among the young and not tolerated among adults. Among an increasing number of blacks and whites, it has meant transaction-based relationships, the end of responsibility for young men, and a skyrocketing illegitimacy rate. Nowhere else in America has the sexual revolution taken so firm a hold as it has among your generation of men and women.

Initially it was by no means certain that these national trends would hit African Americans the hardest. In the 1950s and earlier, the black community had strong moral leadership and a code of cultural norms as firm as any in the white middle class. But during the intervening years, the leadership of these communities made a conscious decision to abandon their obligation to uphold this code. Churches that once served to communicate hope and uphold a moral code have become political action committees. In the struggle against racism, too many of the leaders of these churches, as well as the political leaders, neglected to exercise authority over the community. They were so busy leading the community's march to full equality that they forgot to lead the community. Inevitably others have followed their example. Today few urban schoolteachers would even consider criticizing their students' morals, and, as we have seen, many mothers are often unwilling to correct the young people in their communities. You, Brad, demonstrate as clearly as anyone else that no person or group enjoys any degree of moral authority over the rising generation of inner-city African Americans.

As I am sure you learned from your parents, there are no perfect relationships. One thing that you and your girlfriend need to learn is that you can strengthen each other. You can bring security to each other. Sometimes you can even bring joy to each other. An adult relationship is not easy, particularly when you have children. There will be headaches, and heartbreaks too. Some of your kids won't listen to you no matter how well you teach them and raise them. Like you, they're going to go out there and do what they want to do. Some might even end up with a real tragedy—in jail like your brother or dead like many of your friends. That's the price you pay when you bring children into this world. But if you love your girlfriend as you say you do, you'll find that you can get through tough times. My parents survived a lot of hard times because of the love in their house and in their hearts. It was not a perfect home, but God knew their hearts and helped them through.

More than anything else, your views about women make me worry about your future. You can never completely escape the ghetto unless you reclaim your humanity. That means you have to stop thinking of other people as though they were objects, especially the people who are most important in your life. You have an obligation to treat them as human beings. At this point in your life I do not know if it is even possible for you and your girlfriend to begin treating each other that way, but I am sure that if you do not, neither of you will escape the ghetto or become the kind of parents your children need.

Perhaps the best way to begin is for you to give up sleeping around with other women like some animal. It is the least you owe your girlfriend, and your best hope for yourself and your children.

Sincerely,

Armstrong

Chapter Six

"Everybody Has Kids"

Dear Brad:

I have been very hard on you during my last several letters. As I reread them now, I imagine that you have begun wondering why, if I am so disgusted with your former way of life, I have bothered to write to you at all. Certainly when you first came to me, my initial thought was to dismiss you as just another hopeless street hustler. As we talked, however, I noticed something different about you: you sincerely wanted to do a better job of providing for your children. As I thought about your situation, I realized that if you could stay focused on that one goal, you would find a reason to stay off the streets and the courage to build a decent life. At the same time I knew that if you could achieve your goal, you would be doing more to help the next generation of urban African Americans than all of the social workers visiting your neighborhood combined. Even if things do not work out, for the first time in your life you will have put someone else's welfare above your own. Once you have sincerely pushed your own concerns to the side, you can never go back to being a street hustler. In other words, I knew that by encouraging you to put your children first, your children would save you from the streets.

I must confess that your concern for your children took me by surprise. When you told me that you had three illegitimate children, I immediately envisioned a typical carefree ghetto black man who thought having babies was a badge of honor and impregnating women was little more than an evening's entertainment. But I realized that this was another myth that did not fit the reality of life in the modern ghetto. As you explained, "Most of the guys I know, they're worryin' about their kids. It ain't like they don't care. Most of them try to do for their children." Your assertion was surprising and encouraging to me.

At the same time I was disheartened by the way you defined what it means to be a good father. You proudly boasted that you were able to "provide" for your children when you were dealing drugs. To your way of thinking, "providing" meant nothing more than giving your girlfriend money and buying your daughters gifts. But paying the bills is one of the least important things you can provide for your family. If money were all they needed, the welfare office would be a far better and much more reliable father than you have ever been. It is time you recognized that your daughters need a father, not a checkbook.

As with so many of your other ideas about life, when I heard your definition of being a good father, I shook my head in dismay. I was tempted to ask where you got the idea that a father is someone who pays the bills and stays out of the way. You certainly did not get that idea from your own father, a man who has dedicated his life to his family. But when I turn on the television or open almost any magazine, I stop wondering. As with so many of your other ideas about life, your views about fatherhood are nothing more than an exaggerated version of the popular culture mythology. We live in a culture that condemns men who do not pay child support but says nothing to men who divorce their wives and abandon their children. Even when the president talks about "deadbeat dads," he is referring only to men who do not pay child support. Apparently leaving your wife and children is fine as long as you pay the cable bill.

I am especially concerned that your girlfriend also seems to think the way you do. Like so many other young women today, she has fallen victim to the notion that she does not "need" to be married to be a good mother and her children do not "need" a father. In some sense she is right. Both she and her children are far better off not having you around as long as you are a street hustler. Living with a drug dealer would bring them more danger, which is the last thing they need in their already dangerous world. But your girlfriend should understand that when she decides not to live with you, she is choosing the lesser of two bad options. Being a single mother is not better than, or even as good as, having an intact family, even if it is infinitely better than living with a street hustler.

So, Brad, you must be patient as you try to assume your role as a good father; it will take some time before your girlfriend is willing to take you into her life. You cannot expect to go marching into their house, six years after your first child was born, and announce that daddy's home. If she is a good mother, your girlfriend knows that her first responsibility is to protect her children. In the ghetto that often means keeping her children away from their fathers when they are people like you. You need to do more than make promises to convince her that you have really changed.

At the same time, Brad, I wonder if your girlfriend understands that. If she did, why would she have continued to bear your children after you refused to settle down and act like a decent father? Even as she was condemning you for dealing drugs, she was all too willing to enjoy the fruits of the drug trade—at least as long as she did not risk incarceration and as long as you did not bring the drugs around her babies. In time, I think you will change, and I hope that as you prove yourself, your girlfriend will take you in. I even hope that one day the two of you will get married and give your daughters the kind of family your parents gave you. But even if that does not work out, it is time both of you started thinking about your own daughters. These girls will grow up knowing that their father was a hustler and that their mother raised them with drug money. If she is like most urban black girls, your oldest daughter will begin having sex in just six or seven years. In just twelve years, she will be an adult. With you and your girlfriend as role models, no one will blame her if she hooks up with some street hustler and has babies before she graduates from high school.

I know that judgment seems cruel, but put yourself in your daughters' place for a minute. What will they think about families and raising children? If you and her mother do not intervene, your girls will probably adopt the same attitude that the two of you have. They may believe that all they really want or need from a man is some occasional attention and a regular income to help support their illegitimate children. Should one of your daughters find a good man, she will have no idea how a complete family is supposed to act. Because neither you nor your girlfriend has ever treated each other as a partner, she will imagine that marriage is merely a full-time extension of your relationship with each other. In other words, your girls may well think of marriage as a series of mutually acceptable business transactions in which husbands and wives trade sex, affection, and money as they see fit. Underlying all of their views will be the example that you and your girlfriend have set. The two of you are raising three girls to believe that men cannot be trusted, that fathers are unimportant, and that only money really matters.

I do not need to tell you that even if you set the perfect example, your daughters would have plenty of reasons to adopt that kind of attitude. Most of the young men they meet will be either real or hopeful street hustlers who view women as expensive and often demanding pleasure machines. Few people will blame your girls for not trusting these men or not wanting to make a long-term commitment to them. After a time, your girls will look around and say, just as you said to me, "Everybody has kids." Then, like you and your girlfriend, they might think to themselves, Why not me?

Long before that day comes, Brad, you will have to give your girls an answer to that question. Unfortunately, as your daughters think about having children, they may well see it as the only way to get the type of real love and commitment that all human beings want. They will look around and realize that they cannot get it from men like you. What is worse, if you do not teach your daughters what it means to have a successful life, they will probably believe that having a baby is the only accomplishment even remotely available to a ghetto girl. Your daughters will see their friends becoming single mothers and think that they have found fulfillment through their children. Compared with what most young men can offer them, your daughters will be right: being a single mother is much more fulfilling. By then, it will be too late for you or your girlfriend to intervene. Both your daughters and their children will pay the price, just as you and they are now.

Middle-class parents are often perplexed by the appeal that becoming a single mother to an illegitimate child has to girls in the inner city. I have often thought the welfare system did a lot to encourage this pattern by giving more money to women who had more children. I still think that adds to the problem, but it is no longer the chief cause. You must keep in mind, Brad, that to a girl raised by a single mother, it often seems as if rejecting the pressure to become a single mother herself is the equivalent of admitting that her own mother did something wrong. When any adult suggests that raising children alone is not as good as raising them in a complete family, the daughter of a single mother will often take it personally. Her reaction is to say something like, "I was raised by a single mother, and she did a good job. After all, there is nothing wrong with me." The argument is powerful. Whether she says it to her friends or thinks it to herself, the daughter of a single mother creates a set of false alternatives between criticizing her own mother or rejecting the need for a father. Eventually she will start thinking that she was actually better off without a father. As the number of single mothers has grown, this argument has been repeated so loudly and so often that the daughters of married parents have also fallen victim to it. Today the vast majority of your daughters' friends will have been raised by single mothers, and each of them will make this argument whenever someone challenges them not to have illegitimate children.

Beyond the peer pressure, this argument finds powerful allies in the media. You may remember when former vice president Dan Quayle suggested that the explosion of single-parent families was harmful to children. Practically every celebrity in America criticized his using this same argument. No one was willing to concede the obvious point that, yes, some single mothers do a good job, and their children turn out fine, but it is far more difficult to raise children alone, and even if the children turn out all right, they do not have as happy and complete a childhood as they could have had. That is, I suppose, the politically acceptable response. Since I am not a politician, however, I will be blunt: the children of single mothers usually do not turn out fine.

Your own life demonstrates, Brad, that it is hard enough to keep a child on the right side of the line when you have an intact family with active, concerned parents. As your girlfriend and most of your former associates remind us, when you are raised by a single mother, you are even more likely to wind up in the street hustling. The honest answer to the argument your daughters may one day make is that, no, you were not raised as you should have been. That is why you are looking for fulfillment by having a baby rather than by improving your own life. That is why you find that there is nothing wrong with using drug money to buy things for yourself or your children. That is why you do not respect yourself or the others you know. You can never tell your daughters that when they are teenagers; they will not listen to you. But you can show them that today by giving them the advantages of having a complete, intact family. Then, even if they slip as you have, they will at least know that they are not taking the best path for themselves or their children.

So where do you go from here? Well, Brad, it is time to be a man. You should not expect your girlfriend to take you by the hand and teach you how to be a good father; she probably does not know how either. Instead you are going to have to prove yourself to be a good person and then show her what a good father and a good husband is like. The best place for you to look when you are trying to learn how to do that is to your own father. He has stayed with your mother despite all of the trials you and your brother have put them through. Like you, he was probably tempted by other women, but unlike you, he did not give in to that temptation. Did you ever wonder why he remained faithful? I am sure it was partly because he loves your mother, but then you say you love your girlfriend, and that has never been enough to keep you home at night. Perhaps he has enough self-respect that the solemn vow he made on his wedding day means more to him than the temporary pleasure some other woman might offer.

My own views of what it means to be a good father are

shaped primarily by my memories of my own father. I cannot remember ever sitting down with him and talking about what it means to be a good father and a decent husband, but I knew he was one. He always put my mother and us before himself. That did not mean that he showered us with gifts, and I am not talking about the financial support he provided (although he was always sure that we had enough money to live well). Those are the things you think are important, Brad, but I do not think they ever crossed his mind. Instead, he saw his responsibility as teaching all of us—my brothers and sisters alike—what it means to be a man. He taught us that it means sticking to commitments, even if they are hard. It means having sound principles and adhering to them. It means working hard for financial success but only so you can share it with your family.

My father was never one to use the money he made to buy himself nice cars or fine clothes. When I was young, I used to wonder why. I often wished that he would get nicer things so my friends would know that he was successful. At the time I thought he was just old and out of touch. I figured that he did not realize how much more other people would have respected him if he drove a new Cadillac and wore fine suits to church. But he was not out of touch; he just knew better than I did that those things were not important. He also knew that the kind of respect that those things buy is not real respect at all. The only respect he ever sought was the respect of my mother, and she understood perfectly that it was far more important to be sure I could get an education than that I could ride in a fancy car.

I know it seems trivial to talk about that, but as I have gotten older I find that this is the most difficult thing for most parents to accept. They all seem to be competing with each other to buy their children the fanciest toys, put them up in the biggest house, and give them the nicest clothes. Many of my wealthier friends are no different from you in this respect, so I guess you are in good company. But those wealthy friends of mine can afford to do both. They have enough money to make sure everyone in the neighborhood knows that their children are "rich kids" and they still have enough left over to provide for their future. You don't, and neither do most of the parents that I know. When I see young parents, the easiest way for me to tell how well they are raising their children is to look at the things their kids have. If they seem to have everything the rich kids have, I know that the parents are more concerned with how they appear to others than they are with being good parents. You have to promise yourself that you will never do that.

The money is, of course, only the most obvious sign that parents have their priorities wrong. Underneath the gifts lies an attitude that they are more important than their children. That is what I saw in your description of how you "provided" for your daughters. By giving them things, Brad, parents like you appear to be doing the right thing. Your friends and family will look at the things your girls have, and from the outside it will seem as if you are trying to be a good father. But it does nothing for your daughters. What do you think is important, I mean really important, for your daughters' future? Getting a good education? Staying away from drugs? Growing up to be honest, decent people? Not getting pregnant when they are teenagers? It is probably all of those things and more. But no matter how hard you thought, and no matter how long the list became, you would never include among the things that are truly important to their future "having nice presents when they are young." Yet that is all you have ever tried to give them. And among most of the truly important items on that list, you have actively undermined their future.

How do you become a good father? By doing and thinking the exact opposite of what you usually do and think now.

I know there are many things you will want to give your children and you will think that you do not have enough money to help them, but you are wrong. Even if you do not have a single dollar to your name, you can help them get a good education by sitting down with them each night and reading. You can do more to keep them away from drugs by telling them the truth about your own experience—not the way you told me, with all of your boasting about your power and your money, but the reality of that sort of life. You can set and enforce real rules in your family, not the kind of meaningless rules your parents made for you. But most important, you can show them how decent people live by acting like a decent person yourself. That means standing by your girlfriend and helping her raise the children. It means standing up to your old friends in the ghetto and divorcing yourself from them.

Remember, Brad, it's not important what you say to your children; it's important how you live before your children. Children can spot hypocrisy a mile away; "Do as

I say and not as I do" just doesn't work. By your own actions, they learn what is right and what is wrong. That doesn't mean that they will always do the right thing, but if you raise them to respect themselves and show them that nothing they could do would ever stop you from loving them or caring for them, then there is a good chance that no matter how far they stray, they will make it back safely in the long run.

If you decide to become the kind of father you should be, you will get little or no help from the people around you. Just as they do today, your friends will still measure how well you provide for your children by their toys, their clothes, and the car you drive them in. Your friends will measure your manhood by how well you do with the ladies. And both you and your girlfriend will get constant pressure from the people you know as you try to create and sustain an intact family. If you can just tune them out and do what you know is right, that will be the best lesson of all for your daughters.

Sincerely,

Armstrong

Chapter Seven

"I Guess It's Because I've Never Seen Him"

Dear Brad:

Throughout my letters I have tried to justify living a decent life without referring to God or to religion. I know you do not believe in God, and the last thing I wanted to do was sound like a preacher. When I asked you why you did not believe in God, you told me, "I guess it's because I've never seen Him."

Since we first met, I have thought a lot about that, as well as the other things you said about religion, and I cannot say that I blame you. From your vantage point, religion is nothing more than a preacher standing up on Sunday morning talking about "sin," and church is a place where people your mother's age gather for social visits or where ministers organize the get-out-the-vote drive on election day. If I were in your place, I might also wonder why I had never seen God.

But, Brad, I think you have seen God; you just never noticed Him. There was a time when I had the same doubts you now have. Like you, I began to wonder why God never seemed to show up, especially because I saw that there were so many people who really needed His help. Just like you, my mother told me to read the Bible more, and like you I tried my best to read it and learn how it applied to my life. She raised all my brothers and sisters to pray before every meal, the first thing in the morning, and the last thing at night. To this day, praying is just natural to me. It makes me a person and gives me the humility to understand that I have no power except that granted to me by the Creator.

When we were growing up, my father was a Methodist and my mother a Pentecostal. On the first and third Sunday of each month, we went to my father's sedate African Methodist Episcopal church. It was the alternate Sundays that I loved; we all went down the road to this rocking-and-rolling, foot-stomping, drums, guitar-, and tambourine-playing Holiness church. Even today when I'm home in Marion, I go to that same little church.

But there was a time when I was a teenager that I began to think the Bible was just another book. I had a hard time believing all of those old stories had any meaning for me. It is not so much that I stopped believing in God as I started thinking that He no longer acted in the lives of ordinary people like me. Then I saw Him.

It is not that I had a vision or anything, but I began to see God's presence in the life of others I knew. These people did not fear death as you do; they did not lust for money or power; they did not worry about the little slights and obstacles that you find so irritating. In a word, they were content. At first I did not understand their outlook. They worked hard, but they did not seem to be working primarily to get rich, so I thought they must not understand the power and freedom that came with having money. They would encounter some racist, and instead of getting angry, they would believe that those attitudes hurt the racist far more than they hurt black people. It is as if they pitied racists rather than hating them. Even when they or one of their family members faced death, they were saddened only by the fact that they would no longer enjoy the dying person's company instead of feeling sadness for the person who was dying. If these people had been in your shoes when you were kidnapped, they would have felt sorry for the kidnappers and prayed for them.

These religious people had real power. They could face life and even death with a degree of courage your friends on the street cannot even imagine. I saw that power when I watched Dr. King face down the racists in the South while I was growing up. Every time I read one of his speeches or one of his books, I was struck by how he drew his strength from his religion. I saw fear in the eyes and in the words of the rifle-carrying black revolutionaries like the Black Panthers, but I saw calm confidence in the eyes and in the words of Dr. King. The same Bible I struggled to understand gave him the power to face down the Klan. You can see the same strength in the eyes of Nelson Mandela— twenty-seven years in prison before becoming the president of South Africa. He knows, and he talks about, that it had to be a higher power that put him there.

Now that I have enjoyed some financial success, I know plenty of people who "have it all." They are famous throughout the world, and they have enough money to buy anything that is for sale. But even among people with all of that fame and wealth, I have never met one who is happier than the poor people in South Carolina who truly knew God.

As a teenager I was not sure what to make of these people. Some days I just thought they were fooling themselves. Other days I thought they knew something I did not. Even though I read the same Bible they did, attended the same church they did, and prayed to the same God they did, I started to think they must have some secret hot line to God. But most of the time I just envied them for their happiness. I wished that I could be like St. Paul and have a personal visit from God. Then, I thought to myself, I would find that same happiness. Some days as I worked alone in our fields, I would imagine that God was going to come down and speak to me. If only He would, I thought, then I could really find the kind of peace these people enjoyed. All I needed was just one personal visit, one unmistakable sign, one voice coming from the clouds, to convince me that He was really there and cared about me. The visit never came.

Years later, I thought again about those days when I was waiting for a personal visit from God. My father was very ill, and he had come to George Washington University Hospital to die. I think he wanted to spare my mother the grief of watching him die at home. He was like that until the very end of his life—always worrying more about her than himself. I spent every day for two weeks sitting by his bedside. The doctors said he was in terrible pain, but he never once complained. When he was not too tired to talk, he would ask mostly about me and how I was doing. Both of us knew he had only a few days left, but somehow he did not seem to mind. My father had always been a religious man, and now his religion gave him confidence. He was asking about me and the rest of my family because he wanted to be sure he made his final arrangements in this world before he left it. He knew it would be the last time he could meet his responsibilities.

During the final day, he did not say much of anything. Then, struggling to catch a final breath, my father passed away. He had faced death the way he faced life, with a positive outlook and a confidence that I can only hope to find. As I left his room for the last time, it occurred to me that I had gotten my wish: I had had a personal visit from God. He had been there with my father, giving him the strength to face death. I did not see Him because I refused to notice, but He was there. As I thought about it, I realized that I had seen God many times in the lives of others I knew, and I had even seen Him act in my own life. But until my father's death, I never paid God much attention. It was not that God had not come to me; it was just that I had my eyes closed.

I do not want to just repeat your mother's advice that you read the Bible. Frankly I do not think it would do much good. Sometimes I think Christians use the Bible as a crutch, telling others to read it with the assumption that the whole thing will be obvious if they do. Usually it is not obvious, and besides, I do not think you need to read the Bible to find God. Now don't get me wrong. I firmly believe that the Bible is God's word, but I also know that most of the early Christians in Africa and elsewhere did not have a Bible to read. It is easy enough to tell others about the life of Christ without asking them to "read the Bible." So my advice is different: you should try to live the Bible. Read it later. For now, you probably already know more than enough about it to make a good start.

The harder question to answer is why should you bother trying to live a moral life if you do not believe in God. I can give you one answer, and although it is true, you will probably find it unsatisfying: you've got to put your faith in a higher power, live for something greater than money or houses or cars or fame. If you're living for those things, then you're going to be miserable. Remember what the brothers and sisters had during slavery. They didn't have any wealth, but they had their faith, and that's what brought them through. They understood better than you and I ever will that in the end, only faith is left. Unless a man has his hope and his spirituality, he will die a very poor man indeed.

Brad, I know you want me to give you proof that God exists. I can't. But I can tell you that He acts in my life every day. As I struggle to live the right way, I often find strength I know did not come from inside me. And make no mistake, trying to live the right way is very, very hard. Just try it for a day. Just try to get through one day thinking and acting as if you believed that everyone you meet is a fellow child of God and that you have no right to look down on or judge that person. Try to act for one day as though God Himself had personally demanded that you, Brad Howard, should treat your girlfriend not as your sex-mate but as the daughter of the Almighty. Think about the fact that at the end of the day you will have to face her "dad" and explain to Him why you treated her the way you did.

In some respects I do not even think it matters much whether you believe in God. After all, not believing in God is like saying you do not believe there is such a thing as air: you have never seen it, you would be hard pressed to prove it was there, but whether or not you believe in it, you still have to have it to live, and so does everyone else you meet. So don't believe, but remember to breathe anyway. Act for just one day as if you believed and as if God was watching you, and I think you will begin to notice that He was there all along.

I should warn you, Brad, that trying to live like a Christian is a whole lot more difficult than reading the Bible. It is also a whole lot more rewarding. If you want answers, you will find them in your struggle to live the way you should. That is where Frederick Douglass found answers, and it is where Dr. King, Eldridge Cleaver, and Malcolm X found them too. You will be in good company.

Just try it for one day and then we can talk about the Bible and what you want to know about what it says.

Sincerely,

Armstrong

Epilogue

A Letter to the Reader

Dear Reader:

As you have read my letters to Brad I am sure there were often times when you thought that you would have offered him different, and better, advice. You are probably right. I do not presume to have all the answers for someone like Brad. He has spent nearly thirty years building a life founded on personal gratification and deceit. It will take much more than a handful of letters to help him unravel and rebuild his life, to break the dependency barrier.

In the past three decades Brad has developed a tightly constructed philosophy that can justify his past and his future without guilt or remorse. As I tried to show him in these letters, he has been helped at every step along the wrong path by his parents, his teachers, his friends, the leaders in his community, and he has gotten a big boost from the popular media. However, that fact does not excuse his crimes. For all the things others have done to make it easier for Brad to choose the life of a ghetto hustler, he must still bear responsibility for his actions. To his credit, Brad is beginning to understand that. In this respect, and in many others, he is far ahead of many of the "adults" in his life, people who are all too willing to dismiss his behavior as inevitable or at least "understandable."

I should also confess that as these letters began to take shape I was surprised by their direction. When I first approached Brad's problems I envisioned giving him a "pep-talk" of sorts. I thought I could just explain how I had managed to succeed and give him some of the tools to find a decent job and make something of himself. But try as I might, I never found an appropriate place to begin that pep-talk. Instead, each time I thought about some aspect of Brad's life I kept returning to those basic ideas that have guided him. As I come to the end of this book I am forced to admit that his problems are not, and never were, something that could be cured by a well-educated, well-connected mentor.

That is why I personally find Brad's story so disturbing. What Brad has become is largely the result of following the leaders in our nation. No one ever demanded that Brad act differently. To be sure his parents thought they were doing the right thing, and so did his teachers and others. But telling a young person to behave as he ought to is far different from demanding that he live up to the standards of civility we expect from each other. Our nation sends two distinct messages to Brad: you should act like a moral human being, but we do not expect it from you. It is a message we transmit loud and clear every day. We transmit it in our classrooms when we instruct our teachers to tout the virtues of abstinence and then hand out condoms at the end of class. We transmit it through the afternoon talk shows that provide a forum for the most perverse and dysfunctional segments of our society and imply that they are typical. And we transmit it through the criminal justice system when we refuse to hold teenagers like Brad accountable for their crimes.

If Brad is cynical and suspicious of our institutions it is because we made him that way. Others have wondered what someone from another planet would think of our society if all they knew about us was what they learned from our television and radio signals. In many ways Brad's view of the world answers that question. What does Brad know of religion, for example? If his view were built around what he has seen and heard on television—and it largely is—Brad would believe that religions are run by crooks, crackpots, and child-molesting priests. How often would he have learned about the overwhelming majority of chaste priests or the legions of men and women who have dedicated their lives to ministering to the most needy? Would he have ever come in contact with the writings of C. S. Lewis or the religious writings of Dr. King? Probably not.

In thousands of small ways Brad would have been taught that living a sinful life is normal while living a moral life is an unrealistic ideal. You can blame the schools or the media or the parents or even the sixties counterculture, it does not much matter. There are virtually no places left where the old virtues are held up and morality is demanded. Nowhere, that is, except in the tens of millions of homes where parents quietly and often desperately push against a culture they cannot tolerate. Even as many of these parents find themselves willing participants in many of the worst aspects of that culture, they try to protect their children from it. In the end, I think that is the true challenge of this book: to help Brad become one of those hypocritical parents who demand far more from their children than they do from themselves.

To those of you who share my concern about his future I make the same promise I made to Brad more than a year ago: as long as Brad is willing to put his old life behind him I will be there to help where I can.

"Where I can." It is unfortunate that, even now, I am compelled to use that phrase. I began the previous sentence with the intention of making a sweeping powerful promise to both you, the readers of this book, and to Brad. But even in the few seconds it took to jot down the words I realized that such a promise is not possible for Brad. Instead it requires a qualifier, and the implicit disclaimer "you may well be beyond the ability of me or anyone else to help you." Neither my best intentions nor the best designs of all the outreach programs, mentoring schemes, or government programs can save all of the young men like Brad Howard. We will be lucky to save a few. Our prospects for saving his children are only modestly better.

That said, we still must try—not only for the sake of Brad or even for the benefit of his children, but for ourselves. Ignoring the millions of young people like Brad and his girlfriend diminishes all of us. In doing so we conspire to promote the attitude I have derided throughout this book, the attitude that tells Brad we really do not expect anything more of him. And if Brad is at least partly the product of the excesses of the larger culture, the larger culture is in equal measure becoming the product of people like Brad. When we do nothing to change people like Brad we are allowing their growing influence on our own children to expand unchecked. Changing Brad means helping him make a better life for himself and his family. It is not enough to say we will "stop" him, we must also show our children that our society will reward Brad if he strives to live as he should.

As I noted in the preface to this small volume, Brad is a real person. Since our first conversations I have helped him find a job and I continue to help where I can as he tries to change his life. Whether you believe my counsel is correct or misguided, I would challenge each of you to do the same. As we are reminded each day, within our country there is a nation of Brads who need your help and advice. I especially appeal to the men and women closest to them, who live with them in and nearby their communities, to reach out to these young people. Those of us who, by the grace of God, have escaped the legacy of racism and poverty and now enjoy a comfortable life have an obligation to help where we can. If the tragic life people like Brad lead is not reason enough for you to reach out than remember this: no member of our race will ever find equality as long as Brad represents our people.

Sincerely,

Armstrong

Afterword

by Thelma Howard Williams

My mother died when my sisters and I were very young. I often wondered how different our lives would have been if she had been around. Nevertheless, my father (Armstrong Howard) played both mother and father to his children; we grew up in a wholesome and loving environment. "Papa", as we called him, taught us everything we needed to know and left an indelible imprint on our lives.

My husband James and I set down the same fundamentals for our children. Raising four children from his first marriage and six more of our own was a test of our faith and endurance. Because of our love and commitment, our unconditional belief in God, and a strong work ethic, we prevailed.

Our household was one of hard work, discipline, and routine. We managed a farm and everyone had to participate. Work, school, and church filled our days and weeks. We spent almost all our time together as a family. James and I encouraged and supported those of our children who wanted higher education, even though our schooling ended after seventh grade. We understood, and taught

Armstrong and his brothers and sisters to understand, the value of education in our present day world.

I am proud of all my children. Our family faced difficult challenges, from the Jim Crow of pre-integration South Carolina to the hazards of farm life. However, we overcame these obstacles and continue to thrive. My philosophy has always been simple: If you can take it, you can make it.

We hope this book serves as a beacon of hope to those who have lost their way, and serves to encourage others to continue on the righteous path.

Marion, South Carolina